Love and Death in Lisdoonvarna

Edward Murray

Copyright © 2024 by Ancraic Holdings Ltd

All rights reserved. No part of this publication may be reproduced, distributed, or transmitted in any form or by any means, including photocopying, recording, or other electronic or mechanical methods, without the prior written permission of the publisher, except in the case of brief quotations embodied in critical reviews and certain other non-commercial uses permitted by copyright law. For permission requests, write to the publisher, addressed 'Attention: Permissions Coordinator,' at the address below.

edward.m.murray@gmail.com

This is a work of fiction. Names, characters, businesses, places, events, locales, and incidents are either the products of the author's imagination or used in a fictitious manner. Any resemblance to actual persons, living or dead, or actual events is either purely coincidental or used in a fictitious manner, except when they really were alive.

ISBN: 9798329417166
Imprint: Independently published

Cover by Kathleen Dawson MBE. Kathleen won a Swimming Gold medal at the 2020 Tokyo Olympics. One very talented young lady.

A NOTE FROM THE AUTHOR

This is the first book in the O'Malleys & Kellys series.

I hope you will enjoy the stories and their humour.

My books integrate real-life figures and events with my fictional creations. This book is set in the 1920s and features Catholic theology and practice throughout, although it is secondary to the story.

It is impossible to recreate the wonderous writing of Joyce, Greene, O Connor, Waugh, et al, but this is from where I have taken inspiration.

If you find spelling mistakes and language anachronisms, I would love for you to point them out. But also forgive. The first edition of Ulysses was recorded as having 2,000 mistakes, when the second edition was produced it went up to 3,000 and I note from the link below that the 1984 edition found 5,000 errors.
https://archive.nytimes.com/www.nytimes.com/books/00/01/09/specials/joyce-edition.html

Hopefully, I will not have that many. Albeit, it may not be quite as good.

In addition, please consider leaving a review on Amazon. It makes a difference....

Books by Edward Murray

Murder on the RMS Olympic (September 2023   O'Malleys)

Christmas Murder at the Sacre Coeur (November 2023 O'Malleys)

The Murder of the Devil's Advocate (January 2024 O'Malleys)

Love and Death in Lisdoonvarna (The first Kelly's adventure, February 2024)

The Fourth Secret of Fatima (Kelly's adventure, Spring 2024)

Murder on the Santiago de Compostela Trail (Summer 2024 O'Malleys meet the Kellys)

Primary Characters (in Order of Appearance)

Seamus Carville - The deceased
Jack Kelly - Young American dragged by his father to Ireland to re-discover himself, late 20s
Robert Kelly - Father to Jack, recovering from the loss of wife the year before, late 50s
Maire McDonagh – Landlady of Hotel/Guesthouse
Tom McDonagh - Son of Maire, early 30s
Old/'Oul Dympna - Mystic and keeper of the well. Could be 70, but possibly 80. Maybe even older
Michael McDonagh - Twin of Damian, firebrand early 20s
Damian McDonagh - Twin of Michael, easygoing. Maybe too much for his mothers to like
Sergeant Eric Nixon - Long time policeman in the area, early 50s
Paddy Smith - Long time lawyer of the area, early 60s
Tim Smith - Son of Paddy, smart but directionless, nearly 30
Jonjo O'Herlihy - Pub owner, bon vivant. Fearful for his daughter. Early 50s
Mary O'Herlihy - Beautiful, shrewd daughter of Jonjo, late twenties
Inspector Armstrong - Tough, ruthless operator of Special Branch

Secondary Characters (in Order of Appearance)

Siobhán - Daughter of the shop owner, opposite the McDonagh Hotel//Guesthouse

The Dolan Sisters - Close friends of Siobhán and Mary, mid-20s. Deirdre, Sinead, Breda.

Willie O'Neil - The Matchmaker

Bob McFarlane - Farm owner with an interest in horses

Douglas McDonald - The Resident Magistrate (RM) for Clare

Thomas Dillon - Had been imprisoned after the 1916 uprising, now a professor of Chemistry

Sergeant O'Reilly - Sergeant at Nenagh

The Hotel the Kellys are staying in what could also be called a Guesthouse or Lodging. You have to imagine what the 1920s West of Ireland could offer, particularly at festival time, when every spare room would be taken.

Prologue

Seamus was up early. He had not slept. It was just too warm. He dressed himself and grabbed a towel, it was a bit smelly, but whatever. He would take himself up to bathe in the Kilmoon river, higher up the hill where no-one could see him.

He tramped past the 'Twin Wells' and noted that *oul' Dympna* was not sitting in her usual seat, too early even for her, he thought. Not that there would be many customers at 5 am.

He removed his work boots and gently dipped his toe into the stream. It was rather chilly at first, so he withdrew it. But then he took off his trousers and shirt, and ignoring the initial chill, walked straight into the water. He breathed deeply and settled down as the waters went over his shoulders. That was better. This would keep him going for the day.

He heard a noise above him, a few rocks had slid down the hill, probably one of the sheep, although he could not see it. But it unnerved him. There was a hint of daylight, but no more than that. He took himself out of the river and dried himself, before putting his shirt, trousers, and shoes back on. Why should he be worried? A big man like him, who could lift his weight in bales of hay? Who would be a threat?

He made his way down the hill, slightly unnerved, certain there was someone or something looking at him. As he passed the Twin Wells again, he stopped and looked around. No, nothing. What was he worried about?

Noting that Dympna had left one of her drinking vessels beside the well, he bent down and picked it up. He scooped the water from the bucket and downed it in one gulp. He nearly threw up. Bending down, over the bucket he lowered it into the well, and quickly pulled it up again, filling the cup with the water it had accrued, this time he began to sip. That was better, much better, the first cup of water must have gone off, he thought.

He then heard another noise. Again a few rocks came tumbling past. There was something up there.

"Who are ya? Show yerself." He shouted.

Silence.

Seamus then let out a loud whelp and charged up the hill ten yards, flailing his arms to scare off any animal it may have been.

Nothing moved.

Must be his imagination, he mumbled to himself and made his way back to the village.

As he approached his dwelling, a small thatched-roof cottage on the edge of town at the foot of the hill, he looked around and saw a man approaching him. He could not make out quite who it was, but if this man wanted trouble, Seamus would give it to him.

"Are ya followin' me, ya blackguard?"

There was no response. Seamus stopped and started to move toward the man, which caused the man to turn around and slowly move away.

"I'll have ye, ya hear me, I'll have ye," Seamus raised his voice and a fist.

Suddenly Seamus found himself unable to move, in fact, he was on the ground struggling to breathe and with immense pain in his stomach. He began to gurgle. The man looked at Seamus on the ground as if unsure what to do.

Within a few minutes, it did not matter. Although Seamus's eyes were wide open, he was dead, blood trickling from his mouth.

1

It was still raining.

Did this country do anything else?

Jack stared out of his window from the first floor of their 'Hotel.' It was mid-afternoon, they were situated just off Main Street in the centre of the small town or was it more a village? The big plan for the day had been to go hiking at the Cliffs of Moher, eight miles away.

But that would not be happening now.

It was week two of their trip to Ireland. Their liner, the Olympic had dropped them off in Derry or should that be Londonderry (?) in the North East of the country.

They had spent the first week enjoying a near heat wave and walking the Seven Sisters in Donegal. It was only at the peak of Errigal where the rain had set in, and oh boy did it rain. At the top Jack thought there was a serious chance they would drown such was the volume and ferocity of the lashing. When they eventually slid down the mountain, the rain remained with them wherever they went thereafter as they trundled further south down the West of Ireland.

But now they were in Lisdoonvarna, which as his daddy kept reminding him was one of their objectives for the trip.

Robert Kelly wanted his son to find a wife and settle down. If his son was unable to establish some direction for himself, it was his duty as a good father to ensure it was provided.

But right now the son was looking from the window to his father whose face was half buried in a pillow on his bed. Noisily asleep with a hint of saliva dripping from his mouth.

He most certainly did not look like the master planner, the tough Philadelphian police detective that he presented to the world.

His receding hairline and sagging facial skin scrunched up as his face appeared to bury itself further into the pillow.

Jack decided he would take himself downstairs and go to the shop across the road and have a milkshake. He crept out of the room, managing to creak a floorboard with every step he took. The ill-fitting carpet looked like it had been fitted by a one-armed orangutan and could not be trusted to guide him to the firmer flooring area. His dad though managed to remain asleep. His snoring drowned out everything.

The guesthouse seemed empty, but a small wet brolly was beside the door. Jack put on his mackintosh and opened to turn the lock, stepping outside. Above him, the dark grey skies menaced as the rain came down at an angle banging off the asphalt service road.

Depressing.

Welcome to Ireland.

He skipped across the road and made it to the small shop to be greeted with a huge smile by Siobhán, the young girl who could not have been more than 20 and was working behind the till that day for her father. Her long wispy red hair covered a pale face that brightened up when she saw Jack.

"Well, if it isn't yourself, Jack," she remarked, leaving Jack again having to adjust his understanding of pronouns, third-person pronouns, reflexive pronouns, and singular pronouns all rules of which seemed to have been discarded in her opening line. But as with everybody else he had met since his arrival, he wondered whether it was him (or should he say, 'himself') that was in the wrong?

"Awful day," he muttered back.

"Ah, sure it will clear up later, and anyway, I think O'Herlihy's will open early. Jonjo never misses the chance to grab some custom on these days.

"He must be a millionaire," Jack smirked back at Siobhán.

"He would be if he didn't drink it away," she thoughtfully retorted.

Jack looked at her, she was pretty in a simple way and in some respects was the type of girl that his dad would want for him. She was however he judged, just too young. He was 29, had been to war, and had returned to America, a changed man.

Life was drifting, all his friends, both male and female had an emptiness that the secret speakeasy drinking and driving of fast cars was struggling to fill. They did not want to be conditioned by the older generation that would throw them into a war, casually, and then make tight social rules at its end.

Once you have seen mass slaughter on an industrial scale, you do change.

And yet here he was in Ireland on a tour of Europe in the full knowledge that his dad had a clear subtext. He was to sort his life out....and the finding of a nice Catholic girl was a critical piece in that particular jigsaw.

They were to spend time in Ireland, then Spain and Portugal. Returning in the Autumn of the following year. There would be no visits to France or Italy. They would not return to the past.

He asked for a strawberry milkshake and Siobhán went into the back and came out with it freshly made.

"I was going to put some carrot in it for you, keep you strong for Sunday."

Jack half smiled and then thought, 'carrot?' In a milkshake?

"Well, I am not sure I'll be playing, I've still to hold the hurling stick."

"Oh, you'll be grand. It must be like your baseball stick?"

"So I'm told, Tom in the hotel is taking me out later after he has returned from the field. Although I am not sure whether he will be that interested if he is as soaked as I think he will be."

"I wouldn't worry, it rains most of the time here. If you let rain rule your life, you wouldn't do anything, sure."

Jack nodded in sanguine agreement.

"Well, you could just get drunk,"

Siobhán laughed. He liked her and he knew she liked him, even though he had been there only a short time.

It was as if they had met the whole town. They had arrived early for the 'Lisdoonvarna Matchmaking Festival,' an annual event that had been occurring for seventy years in the autumn.

It had initially been inspired after the famine, *an Gorta Mór* as it was known when because of the sharp reduction in population, the opportunities to socialise with a mass of people when you were from the countryside were limited. Lisdoonvarna had fared better than other settlements and their mythical waters were perceived as being a critical component of this.

Many initially from the surrounding area and then from further afield began to visit the small spa town, bathing in the waters and drinking from the wells and the whiskey barrels, too.

When the Corpus Christi Church was built in 1868, with a hall attached, this became one of the central gathering centres for visitors.

In no time, it became the primary destination for farming fathers to send their sons and daughters to find a partner, all under the watchful eye of the local priests.

They acted as both matchmakers and also moral enforcers. So when the dancing began, they would patrol the perimeter, stepping onto the dancefloor and splitting couples when they were becoming a little too close and then guarding the hills around the town in case a couple had made a break for it, in the hope of finding a little privacy.

Nothing went on without their approval.

This appealed to Robert Kelly.

He liked the order and controlled environment this provided. You did not serve in the Philadelphia Police Department for thirty years without understanding the importance of order.

Siobhán was looking forward to the festival. It was always a lot of fun. Or at least for the two years that she had been allowed to attend by her daddy. She would practice all the dances with her friends and the giddy excitement they felt as the festival approached would be enough to make Vesuvius erupt.

"Have you your eye on any young man, Siobhán?" Jack asked nonchalantly

Siobhán ruefully smiled unsure of what to say, as she looked at this tall dark-haired perfect specimen of an American male who exuded casual confidence.

"That would be tellin,' Jack." She settled for, before adding, "And have you seen anyone you would want to take back to America with *ye*?" Did her voice sound too hopeful, she wondered?

"That also would be tellin'," Jack responded in his attempts at an Irish accent.

More work there needed, he thought to himself, but Siobhán laughed anyway.

"Where does everybody stay when they arrive here," Jack inquired reverting to his normal accent.

"Och, well, everywhere. We will rent out a bed as well at the shed in our back. Even Jonjo O'Herlihy is letting people sleep on the floor of the pub once it closes for the night, mindya,' it sometimes doesn't close when the festival is on," she giggled.

Jack returned the giggle with a smile. Nice girl he thought, but just too young. As he was thinking this, he then began to worry about turning into his father. This would have been what he would say.

Jack had returned from the war in France the year after it had finished. He then suffered the heartbreak of losing his mother, Anne, a few months after that. His father had been inconsolable, and Jack did not have the emotional maturity to help him cope with the loss, whilst also dealing with it himself.

Both men struggled and responded in different ways. Robert, the father found the 'bottle' briefly to help him cope with the loss. This caused him to be nearly sacked from the police department. But strangely the near unscheduled parting from the police eventually helped to galvanise him as he threw himself into his work to fill the void. This left Jack to deal with his own grief. His mother had always been his point of reference. Sure, he loved his dad, but that was a respect thing. Emotionally they were never close. With his mom, it was her that he always wanted to impress. She was the one he went to excitedly after hitting a home run or winning a college football game. As his dad stood with pride when he marched off to a war he did not want to fight in, it was the tears of his mother that would stay with him as he waited to go over the top for the second Somme offensive.

He was a changed man after the war, but at least he had a strong family anchor with his mother being the *shank* on the anchor. But then the Spanish Flu took her, it nearly took Robert as well, but he recovered. She did not.

Jack then spent the next year and a half, drifting. He had a degree in chemistry but had lost all interest in it as he opted to initially work in a bank, but that lasted six months. By the time he had arrived late for the umpteenth time, they dispensed with his services. He tried his hand at insurance, where again his lack of punctiliousness made him a problem more than a help, and then finally after his father had used his influence to help him join the police, he failed in his basic training. And that according to his dad, 'took some going.'

This failure was a tipping point for his father. His 28-year-old (then) son needed to have responsibility thrust upon him. Marriage was the solution in his eyes. But for a marriage to occur it required a suitable prospect and whilst Robert saw many at the weekly Doylestown Masses who would fit the bill, they were not the ones that Jack brought home, that is of course when he bothered to bring them home.

The ones he did meet and sometimes by accident, came in three categories; unacceptable, definitely unacceptable, and 'good grief, what's wrong with him?' In fairness to Jack, he was not looking for a wife, he was looking for fun. He felt that he deserved it. His father had a different idea, and this caused their relationship to be cold and unfeeling.

And thus the idea of a trip to 'oul Ireland' came into shape and then dominated their conversation. Initially, when Robert had raised the subject, it was about re-finding their roots and visiting where Anne had been born. It then metamorphosed into becoming something more. Much more. A trip to Santiago de Compostela and the walking of the Pilgrims Way were added, as was a visit to Fatima in Portugal. This trip was to become an adventure. They could rediscover their faith and as Ireland had been kind to Robert in providing him with a wonderful woman, a wonderful wife when he was Jack's age then Ireland (or Spain, or Portugal) could perhaps do the same for the son. American girls seemed to Robert, at any rate, a bit too interested in fashion, in frivolous things, and in themselves. The old world still retained a hold, he remained firmly of the view, on the important values of family, probity, and strong women who believed in their husbands.

It was of course at this point that Jack's initial interest was put on high alert. Dad had an agenda and although he was not against the agenda, the thought of a sixty-year-old man being a marriage-fixer in a foreign country was not going to cut it.

And yet, and yet....he knew deep down his father was right. He was struggling. A combination of boredom, pointlessness, and a certain restless desire to do something on his terms made him difficult to be with. Unless of course, you were a girl in your 20s or 'one of the boys.' He wanted more, but office life or following his dad into the police was not the solution. Time away would maybe help him find the point of his existence. He needed to move on from the trenches of

France, civvy street in Philadelphia, and hanging out with friends. Maybe this trip was the solution.

Jack thanked Siobhán for the milkshake and noting that Tom had returned to the guesthouse, he made his way out of the shop and ran across to the door, catching it just before Tom had fully closed it.

"You moved quickly there, let's hope you'll be that quick on Sunday."

"Yeah, I was meaning to talk with you about that, Tom."

They both stood in the hallway with water dripping from their mackintosh's.

"Here let's go round back, we're wet anyway. I'll show you how to use a hurling stick."

"Well, I'm not sure I'll be much good, are you sure you want me to play, I'm happy just to watch."

"Och no, you'll be fine," Tom smiled at Jack, sensing this particular reed in the wind needed a little stiffening. He put his arm around Jack and manoeuvred him out to the yard at the back and then to the field behind that again. The rain was no longer pelting down in the manner of howitzer shells hitting the front, it was now a kindlier drizzle.

Tom grabbed two hurling sticks from the shed and gave one to Jack. They were both of a similar age, with Tom being slightly larger in girth and blessed with a redder face. But as he spent most of his life out in the fields, it was unclear whether his complexion was determined by that or genetics.

They stood thirty yards apart in the field. Tom took the *sliotar* (pronounced shlitar) ball from his pocket and threw it into the air and then swinging the stick in a gentler manner than Jack expected, hit the ball in a lob to Jack.

Jack caught it with a nonchalance that surprised him.

"There you go, Jack. You're a natural at this, a natural, I tell ye.'

Jack held the sliotar in his hand. It was similar to a baseball but smaller. It was also slightly smaller than a cricket ball, that Jack had held when playing the game with the British Army in France, in their time away from the front. It was made from cork with a cow skin covering. If you were hit with it, it would most certainly hurt.

Jack copied Tom's throw and then followed through with a swing of the stick. But it was not the gentle swing of Tom. It was more full-blooded. Tom watched as the ball whistled over his head and into the adjoining field.

"Okay, well by the time we find that ball, I think we can call it a day. If you know how to smack the ball, you'll be fine. If you do that on Sunday, Doolin won't know what hit them." He laughed out loud.

It took them twenty minutes to find the ball and during that time, Tom outlined the rules with the critical one being it was three points if you scored a goal and one point if you were able to hit the ball over the bar. Jack would play in the midfield which meant that there would be a lot of running expected of him.

A concern that Jack had, that he felt could not be voiced was just how dangerous was it to be running around a field with thirty people waving sticks. Tom did not seem to think that obvious point relevant enough to mention. He was more focused on the Saturday evening 'hop' at the Church hall. It would be packed with 'lots and lots of girls,' although Tom was concerned the ones he would be interested in would not meet with his mother's approval.

They returned to the house. Tom's mother was waiting at the door with a face of fury. She had spent the past twenty minutes drying up the hallway from when they went through earlier.

They would now be drying and cleaning themselves outside under the mother's watchful eye. She used her other eye for the water on the stove that she was boiling. It was time for a cup of tea.

Once dried they both sat at the kitchen table and were handed the beverage with a slice of soda bread and butter.

There was a knock on the door.

The mother went to the door, it was Sergeant Nixon, with two other officers of the Royal Irish Constabulary (RIC). This was a surprise, nothing had been reported, and none of their guests had done a runner.

Sergeant Nixon asked to speak with Tom who came to the door.

"Well, what about ye'" Tom asked genially.

"I'm sorry about this Tom, but I'm here about Seamus. We've been told he was murdered. And we have a witness that saw you walking near him when he died. In short Tom, you're under arrest."

2

"Who do you think you are Eric Nixon?" The 68-year-old with the crinkled face challenged the 45-year-old who had just as crinkled a face.

"Now Maire, I am only doing my job and if I don't do it, they will send someone across from Dublin."

"Only doing your job? Only doing your job ye'say, arrestin' my Tommy is you being too big for your boots. Yer' da' wouldn't haven't done it."

Tom looked at Nixon sheepishly and shrugged his shoulders.

"I'll get my coat, are you likely to want me for long?"

Nixon looked at Tom with a pained expression, Tom had not fully understood what was being said, despite his mother understanding all too clearly.

"Tom, I'm arresting you. You'll have to come down to the jail and stay there. This is a warrant that has been signed by the Resident Magistrate in Ennis. I don't have a choice. You will have to stay in prison and be questioned by the detectives from Ennis. That will be tomorrow morning. I will ask Paddy Smith to come and see you. He knows how to deal with the detectives."

"Will you be giving me my dinner?"

"Yes, we will be giving you your dinner."

"Oh no, you won't," Maire started again, "I'll be making him his dinner, I wouldn't trust you as far as I could kick you."

"Now Maire, calm down," Nixon pleaded, with zero expectation of success.

"Don't you tell me to calm down, it's people like you that are causing all the problems, and that's why you're going after my Tom."

There were days when Nixon enjoyed his job and then there were days like these.

"Tom," Nixon looked plaintively at the son, "Can you have a wee word with your mum,"

Tom shrugged his shoulders.

"Look Ma.' I'm sure, I'll be back in a few days," Tom then looked at Nixon, "Can you let me out for the game against Doolin on Sunday?"

Nixon looked grave as he shook his head,

"Sorry Tom, I can't do that, I'm sorry."

Tom put on his Macintosh and much to his mother's annoyance did not hug her on the way out, she shouted for him to return and correct the error.

This he did, somewhat embarrassedly, and then walked with Nixon and the two constables to the waiting Wolseley police car. It would be quite a squeeze for the twenty-mile journey to Ennis.

The door closed.

Maire looked at Jack with tears in her eyes.

"D'ya think they'll hurt him?"

"I'm sure they won't and I am a witness."

"They won't care," she remarked before requesting Jack, "Could you go to the field and bring the twins back and call in at O'Herlihy's and see if Jonjo is around? Tell him what they've done. He'll know what to do.

Jack was uncertain whether to disturb his dad and let him know about the events or go and look for the brothers. Maire's reddened eyes made the decision for him.

Jack walked the mile to the field. Tom's younger brothers, Michael (Micky) and Damian (Damo) were sat with four large bags around them. They had been harvesting potatoes from an early crop. Jack approached and told them the news. Micky was particularly angry.

"The 'Tans' are coming after us, I'm telling yez, they're comin,'" Micky immediately offered.

Jack had been warned by his father not to engage in any political talk. Ireland was going through a minor civil war. It was unclear at times who either the good guys or the likely-to-win guys were.

The British authorities had effectively partitioned Ireland, giving the south and the west to a new free state government whilst retaining the North-East as part of Great Britain. An in-built Protestant majority ensured loyalty to the crown for that region.

A messy low-level war had taken place between the British and the Irish Republican Army (IRA) led by Michael Collins, but a ceasefire had been established in the summer of 1921. Those who had been fighting each other were negotiating the terms of the peace and the eventual governance of the island. The Royal Irish Constabulary (RIC) were caught in the middle. It was a police force made up broadly of both Protestants and Catholics and they had been attacked frequently by the IRA. They were then supplemented by the *'Auxiliaries'* or the *'Black and Tans'* as they became known. This was an irregular paramilitary unit made up of ex-soldiers and in some cases ex-prisoners, who caused both fear and mayhem to communities across the land in the name of restoring the peace. They were being disbanded, as part of the ceasefire, but suspicions remained. There was however a period of calm on the island by the autumn of 1921. But the calmness masked the tinder box. There were those in the RIC who wished for Ireland to remain as part of Great Britain, whilst on the Republican side, two very different blocks were beginning to emerge. The first bloc wanted to see only a united Ireland with no connection at all with the British state. Their view was forming that the Protestant majority in the North-East would simply have to accept the will of the majority on the island as a whole. If they refused to accept this, then their consent would be forced. The other grouping would accept a phased withdrawal of Britain and guarantees of rights for the Catholics living in the North-East with British military settlements, specifically military naval harbours at different locations in the South being allowed.

For many of those living in country areas, this debate was moot. They were more focused on surviving and raising their invariably large families. But for some, their politics was their passion, and they could lead many onto unpredictable paths from which they would struggle to return.

Jack walked with the two boys, who were in their early twenties back down the road to the town and past old Dympna who was sitting under a rather weather-beaten umbrella, smoking her small pipe beside the twin wells, everybody acknowledged each other, but no conversation was had. They stopped at O'Herlihy's and inquired from Charlie, the barman if Jonjo was around.

He was.

But he had been 'taken a wee bit with the drink,' and therefore was indisposed. Maybe they should return in an hour.

So they made their way back to the house.

Siobhán was standing outside the shop talking with her friend Mary, the rain had stopped. Temporarily.

Both the twins had told Jack about the mysterious death two weeks previously of Seamus Carville, who was discovered, lying dead with blood and a strange froth dribbling from his mouth, two hundred yards from their house.

Nobody knew what had happened, but the police had arrived with other people who wore white coats. The boys themselves were unsure of what they were doing but had been informed later they were part of a science unit because of the unusual nature of the death.

Nobody thought it was murder, all assumed he had taken too much drink, and his body could not handle it and something inside him burst. You did not need to be a scientist to see that. Apparently. And why would anybody want to kill Seamus anyway? He was harmless, he was soft, he was nearly fifty, which to the twins was very old.

So by the time they joined Siobhán and Mary to chat, Jack had been informed of everything the twins thought pertinent. Michael was the angrier of the two but made a point of calming down when they were with the girls. Both the boys had an eye for Siobhán. Mary was older than them and therefore deemed to be out of their league.

"Any further news?" Jack interrupted the conversation that the girls were having but given that the girls had been talking whilst looking at the three men coming towards them, it was an interruption that was welcomed by Siobhán and Mary.

"No, nothing. Maire is very angry; she has been up and down the street telling everybody that the 'Black and Tans' have taken Tom away." Mary advised.

"But it was the police, wasn't it?" Jack said in mild surprise.

"Well for Maire, they are all the same." Mary rolled her big brown eyes and smiled.

Jack wondered briefly what his father would think about this one, who was more his age and had luscious black hair that swept down her back over the obligatory pale local skin.

He smiled back and nodded his head.

"Sean Maguire has taken the pony to Ennis to inform Paddy Smith, so hopefully Tom will have some legal help very quickly. Paddy will sort them boys out. He takes no nonsense from the police." Mary spoke with the assurance of someone who had some awareness, but a lot less than was needed.

"Well, we can only hope," Jack responded in an agreeable tone.

"We had better go and see your mother now."

The three men turned away and entered the front door, where an initial reaction would have been that there were no issues in this household.

Jack's father, Robert, was sitting at the table with Maire standing over him, he had a very large cup of tea, and in Maire's hand was the largest lump of bread Jack thought he had ever seen.

"My boy is a good boy, it's them Protestants that have done this, if my husband Fergal McDonagh was still alive he would beat up the lot of them for taking my Tom." Robert Kelly nodded in a manner to indicate this fusillade had not just recently started.

"Now, have some more bread and butter and I will refill your cup."

"No, no Mrs. McDonagh, you have been too kind already."

"I told you to call me Maire," Maire said in mild chastisement before continuing, "When Fergal died, the McDonagh name died with him. Except for the boys of course. They'll always be McDonaghs," she beamed. Robert Kelly was not sure whether this was because she had accessed some pleasant memory of Fergal or whether it was because the twins had returned.

Either way, he was relieved and even more relieved when he saw that Jack was with them, he rose from his seat as Maire went to greet her boys in floods of tears.

Jack stayed at the door and motioned his head to his father to come outside and let the McDonagh twins deal with the mother. Robert needed no second invitation and grabbed his hat and coat that were hanging up beside the door and joined his son.

Jack shouted through the door that he would go to O'Herlihy's again and wait for the owner Jonjo, to ready himself before bringing him down to discuss what they should do next.

This would also enable him and his father to have a pint of 'Beamish,' the stout that was served in the pub. Guinness was due to arrive during the week but was late, they would make do with the other for the minute.

Both men were acquiring a taste for the black stuff and were beginning to become a little concerned that they would struggle to wean themselves of it whenever the time came to return to prohibition America.

3

It was later in the afternoon. The 'quick one before going back to the wife for tea' crew had not begun to arrive at the pub. They were still in the fields. This meant the Kelly's were doubling the clientele in the bar.

They walked down Main Street past a menagerie of housing types, adjacent cottages, two-story buildings that were terraced, and then an odd house, sat on its own attached to nothing. Some had painted themselves brightly with green, white, yellow, and a type of gold being the main choices. The older cottages tended to rely on the white, with the local haberdashers, being bright green and the butcher choosing a lively yellow. It was nothing like Philadelphia, it was nothing like small-town America. Or anywhere else on the planet for that matter.

The blue sign with the name O'Herlihys emblazoned on it with the words 'Spirits' and 'Vintner' bookending it could have done with some fresh paint, but then the darkened windows were set against dulling yellow paint, which could also have done with a touch-up. It was a functional pub for functional socialising.

"So what happened?" Robert quizzed Jack.

"Well we had been out back hitting the hurling ball, and when we returned, the police arrived and accused Jack of murder."

"Did they have a warrant?!

"I didn't see Dad, nor did I think to ask. The policeman who arrested Tom seemed to be pretty genial. I'm not so sure about the other two guys who accompanied him. Maire tore into him. They all knew each other, it appeared."

"Well if they did not have an arrest warrant then, we should be able to have him released. Or at least that is what would happen in America." Robert reasoned, then much to his chagrin, Jack began to laugh,

"When would that be Dad? Before or after the guy is shot for trying to escape?" This humour was met with a scowl.

"Son, the Philadelphian Police Department is one of the best in America and the world. And I would add it has fed, clothed, and educated you. So be grateful."

Jack's mind went to the trenches from a few years before and he found himself biting his tongue with wanting to add 'grateful?' For sending me to hell for eighteen months....' He found his mood changing, his Dad still did not understand.

"We have to be able to help Tom. So, we need to know how the victim died."

"Is that not for the police here to investigate?"

"Yes, it is, but we should make our inquiries, the politics here means that justice can find the wrong perpetrator. This does happen in the US as you know, particularly in the South, but we can provide a different eye to help. And that means starting with the owner of this bar. If he is still a little drunk, let's buy him a drink and get his view. Jonjo O'Herlihy strikes me as a talker."

"A talker? Dad, he did not shut up two nights ago when we were here. We could barely hear the music. And it's all hot air. If you think we will get much intuition from him, then I think we are in trouble before we begin."

"That may be so, but it is where we will start," Robert Kelly was standing now and moved to the bar.

"Hello bud," he addressed the barman whose name was Charlie, a point he made back to Robert Kelly.

"Well Charlie, is Jonjo awake yet, we would like to buy him a drink and have a quick word."

Charlie half smiled and looked at the door to the rear of the bar, which was surprisingly well-lit from natural light.

"I'm thinking a drink is probably the last thing he needs, but we do need to wake him up, I'll go and get him."

Charlie returned a few minutes later with Jonjo O'Herlihy following slowly behind.

Jonjo came out having forgotten to comb his hair. He also had forgotten to tuck his stained shirt into his trousers and his undone shoelaces made him an accident waiting to happen. But regardless of all that, his well-fed reddened face and garrulous nature made him a presence.

"So you Americanos, would be wanting to have a word with me?" He looked to Charlie.

"Charlie, they will not be drinking alone in my pub, pour me a Beamish."

O'Herlihy forced his ample frame into the corner table that the Kellys were sitting at. The chairs were more like benches designed to accommodate as many people as they could. The pub was more one for standing in, with seats and tables kept to a minimum. A fresh grounding of sawdust had been added, to help mop up the likely spillages from those who were about to arrive.

Jonjo O'Herlihy smiled as *his* barman brought *his* pint.

"Now boys, what can I be doing for yez?"

Robert acting as an elder statesman looked gravely at Jonjo and told him what had happened with Tom, and was slightly taken aback by Jonjo's initial comment.

"But he's our best player!"

"Sorry, what?"

"He's our best player, we'll never beat Doolin now."

"Dan, he has just been arrested for murder, the hurling match is hardly the issue at the minute and Maire thinks you may be able to help?"

"I'll help him alright; has he been taken to Ennis? Has Paddy Smith been contacted? Who was the arresting peeler?"

The rapid fire of comments and questions by Jonjo took Robert Kelly even further aback.

"Yes, he has gone to Ennis, and I think they said that Paddy Smith would be contacted. I'm not sure who the arresting *officer* was." Robert Kelly would have the job title respected.

"I think his name was Nixon," offered Jack.

"Eric Nixon?"

"Yes, I think so,"

"He's a good sort, it's the ones around him I wouldn't trust or like."

O'Herlihy put his hand on his chin as if trying to access the analytical part of his brain.

"Now let me see, it's Wednesday today, if Paddy can see him later and talk to Nixon, then that would give us two days to sort out bail."

"They will not allow for bail for anyone accused of murder," Robert (un)helpfully advised,

"Well, they have in the past when it's been an obvious made-up charge, and with due respect to Seamus, the man took so much drink, I'm amazed he lasted this long." Said the man with a girth that could support four fetuses.

He looked to the bar and signalled for Charlie to come over.

"Charlie, I think Tim will be in the pub in the next half hour. Do not serve him a drink, fetch me and we will drive to his Dad's and then onto Ennis."

Charlie nodded, the Kellys looked on in bemusement.

"Sorry fellah's, Tim is Paddy Smith's son. We will go to Ennis within the hour, and I will make sure that Paddy is talking to Tom, to Eric and also the Resident Magistrate for the area," he paused as if summoning up his strength, "The Resident Magistrate, Douglas Theobald McDonald," he paused again and looked at the Kellys, "Aye, you're right, he's not a local." Adding a half smile.

Much to Jack's surprise Mary wandered into the pub and sat down beside them.

"So what have I interrupted?"

"I'm going to go to Ennis, I'll take Tim in case Paddy is still in his bed, he can drag him out and see what we can do about this Tom business."

Mary shrugged, "Someone saw him near the body before it was discovered, according to Siobhán, Officer Nixon looked very embarrassed. Although she wasn't sure if it was because of the two other policemen with him, who looked like 'tans, or maybe it was the first time they had ever dealt with Maire," Mary smirked.

Jonjo smiled at Mary's smirk.

"No idea who it was that said they saw Tom?" Robert Kelly inquired.

"No names, but Maire has her thoughts. In general, if you are Protestant or are Catholic and do not go to Mass five times a week, then you are top of her suspicion list. And when she went through the names earlier, it seemed to cover half the town." Maire smiled at Robert, before snatching a glance at Jack and then demurring her eyes away. Something, Robert picked up on, even if his slow thinking, slow acting, would not know a good one if she danced on his forehead, son may not have done.

But he had.

4

Dympna adjusted her stone seat and re-lit her thin pipe. Business was slow, next week however it would lift off. New arrivals from all over, even some from America and Canada would be relying on her to pour them the magical spa water of the twin wells. 'Her' water had iodine, sulphur, magnesium, and iron in it. Apparently. Well, whatever it had, it was truly mythical. Leprechauns, fairies, and the folklore of Aibell, the fairy queen, of Cailleach, whom Dympna secretly admired the most, of Gráinne who placed the *geis* on Diarmuid, to ensure his love were all contained in *her* waters. That was why she had a duty to protect this well and ensure only the right people who respected these mystic properties took the water. In practice, that meant anybody who had a sixpence, which was everybody who requested it. But it kept her comforted in knowing that she was the protector.

Yet she had some residual anger. One of her drinking vessels had gone missing a couple of weeks before.

There was a thief in the village, yet no-one least of all the policeman Nixon seemed to care. She would have to rely on the spirits for justice.

What annoyed her most was she had spent some of her mystically earned money on a new cleaning fluid that Brendan McManus had sworn would make the water taste even better. Well, she wouldn't be talking to him again. Her hands had come out in sores, blisters, and burns the day after she had used it. If she saw him again she would give him a bit of her mind. And ask for her money back. No doubt he would disappear, back to the big city in Cork.

Thankfully though, Jonjo had agreed to give her some of his old drinking mugs. They were a bit grotty, but why would that matter when the people were drinking the charmed water from the twin wells?

She puffed on her pipe and attempted to rock up and down whilst sitting on her stone. For a brief second, she thought she was back in her tiny 1-roomed cottage at the other end of town, in front of the fire sitting in her rocking chair, eating her potato. It was a good life she thought to herself. The downs of the missing cup and that criminal Brendan McManus, she would let go, for the minute.

"Talk to Dan, you're not staying."

"Whaddya' mean, I'm not staying?"

Charlie pointed to where Jonjo was sitting with the Kelly's in the corner,

"You'd better ask him."

Tim Smith made his way to the crowded table for what was now becoming a crowded pub.

"Why can't I have a drink, what's the craic, Jonjo?" A still disconcerted Tim interrupted the group, before apologising to the two strangers and smiling at Mary.

"Because we are getting in your car and going to your Dad's, then from there to Ennis."

"Ennis? Ennis? Why are we going to Ennis?"

"Have you not heard?" Jonjo continued before giving the bewildered Tim a chance to answer, "Tom has been arrested," and then added, "For murder."

"For murder? Tom? Who has he murdered? Are you joking?"

"Nope, and that's why we are going to your Da's right now," Jonjo O'Herlihy lifted his large frame and began a ballet-like movement to eject himself from his seat without upending the whole table.

"And, *by the by's*, this is Robert and Jack Kelly. They're from Amer-ree-kay."

Tim acknowledged the two men, and they returned the nod of the heads. But no conversation was likely to be possible as Jonjo was pulling the blond wavy-haired son of Paddy away in the direction of the bar door and Tim's car.

"We'll call into Maire's when we've returned, it will probably not be too late, but we will call in,"

Tim attempted to say goodbye to Mary but was being dragged too quickly out of the pub to make it as effective as he wanted it to be. This was not good, Mary sitting with another fellah, was never good.

After they had left, Mary smiled at the Kellys.

"My Da' is a force of nature, isn't he?"

"Jonjo O'Herlihy is your father?" Robert asked with his eyebrow raised.

"Oh, aye, that he is," a beaming Mary responded.

Robert attempted to be as diplomatic and polite as he could be, as this was not quite what he was hoping for.

"Yes, what a great guy, he sure reacts quickly, if I may say." He paused then unsubtly switched the conversation, "You seem quite different from him," he furrowed his active eyebrows, Mary responded by laughing.

"Oh I know, I look like me' Ma,' God rest her," she looked to the heavens as she said this but retained a smile. Robert Kelly looked crestfallen.

"I'm sorry, I did not know. Please forgive me."

"Don't worry, she passed on when I was young. I'm used to having Da,' or Jonjo. Even I call him Jonjo more often than I call him Da. He is just a wonderful man. Once you know him."

"My dad's the same," Jack piped in, then added, "Once you know him," Mary shared the laugh at Robert's expense with Jack.

And looked at him again.

"What must it be like to be Jonjo O'Herlihy's daughter in this town?" Jack inquired.

"Well, there is never a quiet moment, even in the quiet moments." Her face seemed to have a permanent smile creased on it. Jack was becoming enchanted; his dad had fallen in love. But not in the romantic sense. And just could not help himself as he heard the question being asked by a person using his voice,

"Does being the daughter of Jonjo not intimidate young people of your age?"

Mary looked at Robert strangely with Jack wanting the ground to open up and swallow his father, followed closely by him, he could feel his pulse racing with embarrassment.

"Well, half the fellah's want to marry me, because they think I'm pretty," she said nonchalantly, "While the other half want to marry me because me Da' owns a pub," she grinned, before adding, "So the former are too shy to talk to me and the latter will turn into drunks, so you're kinda' right, but I will meet the right person eventually. And if I don't, I love my Da' too much to leave, anyway."

"You're an amazing girl, your father is very fortunate to have you," Robert sounding thoughtfully solemn like he was the Oracle of Athens, making the conversation to Jack's ears even more gruesome.

"I'll be grand, I'll dance with a load of boys over the festival and bring a couple of them back here to scare the bejeezus out of me' Da.' And that'll be fun."

Jack could not help but laugh. This girl had palooka. Robert found himself completely disarmed; the girl was as much a force of nature as her father. Yet, very, very different.

"Do you have any brothers, Mary?" Jack asked innocently.

This was not the harmless question, he had assumed it to be, Mary's smile slowly disappeared.

"I did, but the *wars* took them,"

"I'm sorry, I'm so sorry for asking,"

"You won't have known, Da' just has me. And Charlie. And Gerry," she looked at the barmen, "To help run the pub."

The conversation had grounded to a halt. So to lift things, Jack switched the subject to the hurling match with Doolin on Sunday.

"Are you coming, Mary? And do we have a chance?"

"They'll be as rubbish as we are, you're playing aren't you, Jack?"

Jack looked a little sheepish, the wording of 'rubbish' with the name 'Jack' in the same sentence was probably not where he thought the chat was heading.

"Sorry Jack, I didn't mean you, but we are both small towns, so there are not a lot of players to choose from. The fact that Tom asked you to play, when you've only been here two minutes would maybe tell you something," she smiled that wholesome smile again.

Back on an even keel.

"Da' is managing the team, but he only stopped playing a couple of years ago, that should give you an idea about the standard. So I will have to go anyway."

"Will the pub be shut?"

"Well, the team is going to get changed in here, but we will keep the bar shut. Most of the team would arrive drunk if he opened the bar before the game. But it will certainly be open afterwards. I'll be working with the boys; it'll just be mad. Do you fancy working on Sunday night, Jack?"

Jack laughed, then looked at his Dad and laughed again. His dad began to laugh as well. They looked at Mary. She was not smiling.

"I'm serious, Jack. You'll be sober. None of the rest of them will be, least of all, Da'. I could do with the help."

"Am I allowed to?"

"Oh don't worry about that, we can sort out the paperwork later." The wholesome smile was being replaced with a more strategic grin.

"Well, if you need me to help, sure. Maybe, Dad, you could also help," Jack saw no problem in lobbing a grenade into his father's hands.

"Oh, I'm not so sure I would be any good, son." Robert looked at Jack with an edge, before Mary intervened, a little to Robert's disappointment.

"You're probably right Robert, but thanks anyway for offering," the whimsical smile returned.

Jack was able to hide his smirk.

Much to both Jonjo and Tim's surprise, Paddy was not at home. He was in fact already in Ennis, talking to Police Sergeant Nixon and then to his new client, Tom McDonagh.

It took them an hour to arrive in the county town and they went straight to the police station. It was known to both men for different reasons.

Paddy Smith was sitting in a seat with paper on his lap, he appeared to be reading through notes. He looked up with mild surprise when they entered the building.

"What are you doing here?"

"We've come to help."

Paddy looked over his small horn-rimmed glasses. His receding hair seemed to recede a little more by this offer of support.

"Well, there is nothing for you to do. They're releasing him now; all charges are being dropped for the minute. So, you can go home."

Jonjo O'Herlihy who secretly did not much like Paddy Smith - too smart and smarmy for his liking – also preferred to have him on his side rather than against. He had seen Paddy challenge the police, challenge the Black and Tans, challenge the IRA. He was a brutally judicious man, who believed in the meticulous implementation of the rule of law who liked the odd drink.

Yet, yet.....the smarminess was something Jonjo struggled with. But right now, he was gratefully accepting it. His star player was about to become available for selection again.

"Why are they releasing him? If Nixon himself came to arrest him, they must have something."

At this point, Sergeant Nixon came through the door.

"He'll be ready in ten minutes; we are taking his fingerprints."

"Why would *yez* be doing that, he has committed no crime?" Paddy Smith challenged the Sergeant.

"I have to, orders from Dublin."

"You arrest a man based on what a drunk says, who has now withdrawn their statement, and that gives you the right to take his prints? Something not right there, methinks."

"You can 'methinks' all you like, Paddy, I could keep him in, as you well know."

"I know you can Eric, but I also know you. And this is not you. Where is the pressure coming from?"

"Be on your way, Paddy, we can talk another day, it's after 7 in the evening and we both want to go home."

Paddy Smith nodded in agreement; it was late. He looked at Jonjo and his son, Tim,

"You take him back in the car, tell your mother Tim, I'll be home at 9. I have Bessie out the back."

"Da', it's late, why are you taking the pony and trap back at this time? It's gettin' dark."

"I would sooner trust Bessie to get me home safely than you driving the car," Paddy Smith raised his eyebrows and stood up. As he was doing so, Tom McDonagh was escorted through to the front desk with his handcuffs removed.

Jonjo looked as relieved as he was delighted. Tom beamed on seeing Tim. They were friends, of sorts. Just quite different people.

"Does me mammy know I'm coming home tonight," inquired Tom.

All the men shook their heads.

"Well, this will be a nice surprise for her, I hope." He smirked.

They walked out to the parked Sunbeam Tourer; it would be more of a squeeze at the front than the back given the size of Jonjo and Tim. This was maybe another factor in Paddy's decision-making.

Jonjo turned the crank and the engine started, he then moved at a speed that suggested a lightness of foot that was not displayed in any other area of his life. It was as if he thought the car would move away without him. They waved at Paddy as he mounted his 2-man trap. Before taking the brake off, he lit the lamp at the front of the trap and the one in the rear. Paddy Smith did not like cars, he had one because he could afford it, he did not like driving, but a country-based lawyer needed to be able to move around and sometimes, *sometimes* he needed to use the car. Yet somehow, his preference and trust was always with Bessie.

He released his handbrake, Bessie's head slightly turned.

"Aye, me girl, we don't need to rush, let's be gentle and I'll serenade you home," he began to whistle. It was a tune he had heard at the Gaiety Playhouse in Dublin when he was there six months previously and had taken in the stage play 'Shameen Dhu.'

The whistling changed and were replaced by words,
"Too-ra-loo-ra-loo-ral,
Too-ra-loo-ra-li,
Too-ra-loo-ra-loo-ral,
Hush, now, don't you cry!
Too-ra-loo-ra-loo-ral,
Too-ra-loo-ra-li,
Too-ra-loo-ra-loo-ral,

That's an Irish lullaby."

For Bessie, it was a long, long trip home.

5

Maire burst into tears as Tom entered the house and rushed to hug him. Then quickly reverted to form, by shouting at him for having been arrested. Damian calmed her down, a little.

"Ma, he's back again, give him a minute."

The Kellys looked on slightly askance at the cameo that was being played out.

"He shouldn't have been arrested, if my Fergal had been here...." Her voice trailed off,

"Well he's not and he's home, so maybe a bowl of broth would be helpful for him." The Kellys noted that it was Damian who seemed to have taken some control of the house. Tom had remained quiet, whilst Michael was brooding with anger.

"Why do they say it's murder?" Robert Kelly inquired.

"The body had an autopsy done, they cut open Seamus's body, and he was poisoned," Tim responded.

The older Kelly nodded and then thought he could put everybody's mind at rest by advising on what normal police procedure would be, nobody appeared to be listening. This forced him to change tack and he asked how Seamus had been found, Tim responded.

"Dympna found him early in the morning, she knocked Jonjo up and he then roused Gerry, the barman who went to Doolin to find Constable Duggan. Anyway a few hours later,

Nixon and a mob from Ennis were here. And that was it. We did not hear a thing until Tom was arrested."

"Did Seamus have any family?"

"Seamus did not have any family we were aware of; he was a bit of a loner. He's only been in Lisdoonvarna for a few years. I think he was originally from Donegal. But he may have upset a few people there so came south to work in the fields."

"So no obvious motive for anybody?"

"No, none at all, he would sit in the pub and occasionally play the *bodhrán* (pronounced bor-an) at Jonjo's. He was cheerful enough, everybody knew him. No-one though was particularly close to him."

"Seems very strange, did Nixon say what the cause of death was?"

"Well, and I quote my father here, 'it was a very sophisticated arsenic poison,'"

"Well, that would help rule our Tom out." Damian looked at Tom as he said the last bit. They both grinned.

"Did Sergeant Nixon say who had witnessed Tom?"

"No, Paddy asked him as well, but he said that was confidential, the individual claimed later to have been mistaken."

"All very strange. If there has been a murder committed, then I expect they will want to interview everybody in this town."

"Nixon did say that, but they were waiting for extra help from Dublin, he expects them to be here by Monday, so this place will be crawling with police. But at least that will be after the Doolin game." Tim smiled at this, he was playing centre half-forward and likely to be amongst the points and goals – the star position.

"How many of them are coming over from Dublin?" Michael asked aggressively.

"He didn't say, and don't you be kicking off when they're here," Tom answered, asserting control over his younger sibling.

"I'm not going to be slapped around by the 'tans, you may buckle, I will not."

"They're being disbanded, let's have some peace, Michael. Don't be kicking off, ya hear me? Don't."

"You listen to your brother Michael McDonagh. I don't what you going the way of Aiden O'Herlihy.

Jack's ears pricked up at this, as did his father's.

"Was that Mary's brother?" He heard himself ask out loud.

Michael and Tom's argument had been usefully interrupted and Maire seized the opportunity to make this a learning point for her youngest son.

"Aiden was killed in the uprising, whilst his brother was in France."

"What?" Robert heard himself asking askance.

Tom took up the story, he would articulate his mother's point for Michael better than she could.

"Jonjo had two sons, Jimmy, and Aiden. Jimmy was the oldest, and when John Redmond asked for Irishmen to join up and go to the front in France, '*as far as the firing line extended*' he responded. And then died at the Somme. Aiden went the other way; he was always interested in the Irish Republican Brotherhood (IRB) who were against the war and wanted Britain out of Ireland. So when the uprising took place in Easter 1916, he fought with the IRA and was killed the following year."

"Jonjo hates the violence, he hates the British, he hates the IRA, he hates them all. He never understood why both his boys thought this was something worth dying for. He always says that life is hard enough, so why go looking for trouble?"

Jack Kelly listened, and this resonated with him. He was never entirely sure why there was any desire within him to join up for the slaughter in France. How was he to know? And then for what? Friends died, sometimes in bits.

Then there was the killing. He remembered the first time that he killed a man. Shooting at the trenches was not proper warfare. It was bayonet to bayonet, they had overrun the German position on the Somme, they were engaged in hand-to-hand fighting, Jack had been rushed from the side, but the soldier missed. Jack turned and drove his bayonet into the solar plexus of a boy....literally a boy, whom Jack doubted was even eighteen. The eyes of sadness, aware that he would never see his mother and father again before he slumped into Jack's rifle nozzle, dead, would stay with him forever.

After this Jack transferred to the artillery.

He knew why the sons wanted to fight and he also now knew why Jonjo hated the pointlessness of it all. This pointlessness lasted beyond the war. Everything Jack did lacked meaning now. He was lost, hearing the story of Jonjo O'Herlihy's boys told him, being lost was the safer place to be.

Jack was knocked out of his thoughts by his father, with a gentle nudge. Robert knew the look; he had seen this happen before in his son. He knew. That's why the trip to Ireland, to Europe, was important. It was for his boy, his lost boy.

"I'm sorry," Robert started, "But somebody must have seen something or somebody close to the body. They are hunting for someone. May I suggest you all have witnesses available for when you are interviewed." Robert felt he was a good detective, but he had not been averse to using strong-arm tactics when it suited him. He imagined something similar could be applied here, yet....yet, the dead individual was not an obvious person to murder. He did not have a family that the locals were aware of or a core group of friends from what it seemed. And it was a small town, a village even. All very strange. Robert resolved to talk with Paddy Smith when he saw him, which would probably be at the game on Sunday.

Tim returned home in the father's car, and the Kellys finished with a Horlicks freshly made by Maire. They sat around the dining table talking about Sergeant Nixon, Seamus Carville, the lack of any family connection in the area, and the game on Sunday.

It felt like an extended family gathering. Which was very different from what they were used to back in America. At home in Doylestown near Philadelphia, if you were in a hotel everything would seem more formal, clinical even. At this 'hotel,' you were part of something that had no formality attached to any convention. You could be a king but would be treated as if you were the same as a peasant. And vice versa.

Robert found this charming, but as he settled down with Jack in their beds, he shared a thought with his son,

"I think we should talk with Dympna tomorrow and try some of her magical water."

"Agreed, Dad, agreed."

6

The Kellys thought they were up early, but Dympna had already passed the house an hour before according to Maire, which would have been 6 am.

She lived at the top of a hill in an old crofter's shack. Which had been her mothers and presumably her fathers. But no-one seemed to quite know. The roof had caved in a few years before and men from the village put a temporary cover on. The 'temporary' had become the 'permanent.' Whilst efforts had been made to replace it, Dympna had always been difficult. It was more than good enough for her and if truth be told, she did not like people knowing her business. She was a mystic. Mystics tended not to last too long if everyone knew their business. The stones and mortar remained strong in the house, but the remaining element of the roof looked as though it could collapse at any time. It also leaked, but that strangely seemed of little issue to the *mystic*.

She was sat in her usual stone seat with ten drinking vessels proudly displayed at her feet. She wore the shawl, as she had done for forty years. It had been her mother's and although she had no children of her own, she hoped to hand it over to another eventually, who displayed the mercurial knowledge that only she could see.

Banshees were like that. They were the only ones who could see the banshee in others. Regrettably for Dympna though, there were not too many who were displaying the characteristics that could qualify them for her role. Some days she did worry that her shawl would not be handed on to another.

She sat back on her stone and re-lit the pipe as the two strangers from America walked up *her* hill. To *her* well.

"So you would be wanting some of my water, then?"

"Yes, indeed we would, and some conversation if you have it to share," Robert asked as genially as he could, Jack grimaced, his dad had sounded more wooden than the hull of a boat.

"I gather you knew Seamus Carville, it was really sad, what happened to him."

Dympna merely nodded, how little these two from the new world knew.

"Did you talk to him much?" Robert was testing his geniality to its limits. And then a bit beyond.

"Would yez be wanting some water?" Business came first for Dympna.

Robert smiled at Dympna and then at Jack, she had sized them up, quickly enough,

"Yeah, sure that would be very kind, here's a sixpence for your trouble." Robert continued smiling as he handed over the money, he moved to sit on a stone beside Dympna. Dympna put down her pipe and produced two drinking vessels, that were not quite cups and not quite glasses. The dirt had been ground into them. She bent over the well and scooped the water using a ladle before pouring it into the vessels. She handed the first cup to Robert, before bending down again for the second scoop. Dympna did this without exchanging a word with her 'customers.' Once completed, she returned to her seat, picking her pipe up again and slowly relighting it. Her world, her rules.

"So, you wanted to know about Seamus?"

Robert Kelly reverted to his geniality mask.

"Yeah, it must have been quite a shock to find him, just lying there."

Dympna eyed them suspiciously, they did not understand 'the ways,' of life.

"Aye, that I did." She nodded.

This was not going to be an 'easy' casual conversation.

"I gather one of the barmen at O'Herlihys had to go for the police after you alerted them."

"Aye, that he did," she again nodded. Robert shared her nodding head, Jack listened and wondered how his dad was going to move this conversation on.

"Seamus did not seem to have any family,"

"Aye, that he didn't."

"But he was well-liked, everybody speaks well of him, what did you like most about him?"

Dympna turned her head oddly toward Jack rather than Robert. It was a strange question, was his father okay?

"I'm not one for the likin' or the dislikin' she murmured.

Robert's geniality was draining her now, so Jack decided to throw a question in.

"Are you not worried that the police from Dublin will want to talk to you on Monday, it might mean you have to leave here for a bit."

"Why would they do that? A man's dead, nothing more to say."

"Have you not heard? They thought Tom McDonagh killed him."

She shrugged, as if this information was of no relevance to her, before surprising them,

[53]

"He shouldn't have followed him."

"Sorry, 'shouldn't have followed him,' how do you mean?"

"He shouldn't have followed him," she repeated. "No business to follow Seamus. No business at all." She puffed her pipe to conclude the sentence.

"So, you think Tom didn't like Seamus?"

"No, I didn't say that, and don't be putting your words in me' mouth,"

"I'm sorry Dympna," Robert hastily responded, "It just seems all so peculiar, one minute Seamus is walking down the hill, and the next, he is dead."

"Aye, that it is," Old Dympna was returning to her standard refrain.

Robert sighed, whilst Jack was secretly enjoying his father's difficulties.

"He had his demons, that'll be what will have killed him."

"Demons?" At last, thought Robert Kelly, she was opening up.

"Aye, the Púca fairy demons."

Jack nearly burst out laughing, where was Dad going to go with this? Robert Kelly was scratching his chin he had no idea either.

"These demons, these Púca do they take any human form?"

"Aye, that they do when they want, other times they come in the form of wild colts, with chains hanging about them." She looked through the Philadelphian detective as if in a different world.

"Are there any living in the village?"

"Not now, not since the demon left Seamus."

"How do you know; they were in him? How did you know they left him?" The older Kelly had moved past geniality and was hovering in the direction of exasperation.

Old Dympna took her pipe out of her mouth and looked dubiously at him as if he had asked the stupidest question ever in the world of stupid questions,

"He stole the waters and the Púca punished him. If it had been the *Kelpie*, he would have been devoured instead." Old Dympna was talking to errant children.

"He stole the waters," She repeated, then returned to her pipe, murmuring to herself.

The Kellys nodded but were just not quite sure what they were meant to be agreeing with.

"Well let's not take up any more of your time, Dympna," Robert Kelly was giving up. He rose from his stone seat and dusted himself down. Jack was also standing up now. Dympna was looking away, toward the hills and the spirits.

"Have a great day, and that sure was great water. Hopefully, it will give us the good spirits and not the Púca or the Kelpie," Dympna did not bother to look at them as they trundled down the hill again. She was in a different land.

When she had seen Seamus taking the water and then dropping down dead, twenty minutes later, she knew the local Púca had spoken. But how could she explain that to these mortals? They could never understand.

The Kelly's were at the bottom of the hill, when Robert looked at Jack,

"I need a drink," he changed direction toward O'Herlihys. "God help the police with that one."

7

The day of the big match had arrived, but as it was Sunday, it was off to holy Mass first. The Church was full with the Priest, Fr. Enda Donoghue having a permanent smile on his face for its duration. His sermon was on 'fair play,' he liked to keep his sermons relevant and engaging. He prided himself on it.

So he talked of the hurling match as the very embodiment of the new Ireland. Where the old traditions such as hurling would be central to the re-birth of a new Catholic land.

When the team from Doolin arrived, the contest would show the best of this new Ireland. Where good play, sportsmanship, and common Catholic decency would be on display for the world to see.

More importantly, though, God would see. He saw everything, he saw the goodness on the hurling pitch as he saw the goodness in our souls. So when these thirty men stood to play, they stood for Ireland, they stood for Jesus, they stood for the Church.

The Mass ended and the congregation dispersed, with a significant male element moving toward O'Herlihy's. Which would now be open for them.

The Kellys returned to their lodgings, with Tom being particularly keen to make sure that Jack had fully understood the rules. And it would be fair to suggest that Jack was not entirely certain and slightly put out that it was Tom who had taken his arm at the end of the Mass and not Mary. Their eyes had met, he had hoped to have a chat with her, but that was not going to be....

"Keep remembering every time you have the ball, you have to touch it with the hurley," Tom illustrated the move effortlessly and then handed the ball and hurling stick to Jack to do the same. By the eighth time Jack had mis-controlled it, Tom gave it up as a bad job and settled for the more traditional direction given to hurling novices.

"Just smack the ball in the direction of goalposts. And clatter anybody who goes past you."

Jack unconvincingly nodded. Well, at least he now knew a couple of rules.

The Doolin team and its supporters arrived in a variety of cars, and bicycles with several pony and traps full of people. Both teams changed in the pub before walking the ten minutes to the pitch.

Preparations had been made with wood cut to make up the goalposts, which were placed twenty feet apart and then the bar positioned ten feet above the ground. The poles were weighed down with turf bags. Jack had played college football so noted the similarity with the gridiron posts which were slightly less wide, but the bar placed at the same height. The other sports that Jack was aware of but had not played, had slightly different posts. Gaelic Football had an eight-foot bar, which was similar to the other football, soccer, which also had an eight-foot bar, but with wider goalposts.

Jack had met all his teammates but was most surprised to see who the goalkeeper was......Fr. Enda. He wouldn't see fifty again or even for that matter, sixty.

Tom was the team captain, Jonjo O'Herlihy was the token 'manager' because he allowed his pub to be used for changing, but he was never going to be allowed to do the team talk. Both teams limbered up by doing a little disorganised running and then *pucking* the hurling ball to each other. Jack had never heard of the word. However, it simply meant striking, throwing, or hitting the ball with the stick. But every four steps, he was reminded again, he needed to puck the ball, when he had it and had not passed to a teammate.

Jack was becoming less confident by the second.

Tom called the team together and did his pep talk.

"You know your positions and you know they humped us last year. So we will be wanting revenge. Jonjo might even give us a free drink. Now we have to protect Fr. Enda in the goals and use Jack maybe for dummy runs. Nobody is allowed to get injured even if they take your head off."

This point moved Jack's rapidly disappearing confidence into overdrive. He now had fear.

The referee called both team captains together, to toss the coin for which end of the field they would begin the game. As the sheep had spent the week eating the grass to keep it low and remove the rougher weeds, the pitch itself looked nearly manicured. There were several flag sticks around to mark out the rectangle of the pitch. Several men wearing white placed themselves behind the goals for when the sliotar went out of play. Given that the Doolin team were in white, mainly collarless shirts, Jack wondered whether this may cause some confusion.

Lisdoonvarna wore dark colours, with a disproportionate number of dark waistjackets making up the attire.

Tom won the toss and maintained the side of the pitch they were warming up on. It was a slight downslope that they would face up to. He figured that the second half would be when they would need the downslope the most.

The referee shouted for all the players to ready themselves and the crowd to stand well away from the pitch. But as it was five deep that request was not likely to hold for too long.

Jack could make out his dad and he thought he could make out Mary, but she seemed to be surrounded by several pub regulars who had all said goodbye to fifty years of age.

The referee blew his whistle and threw the sliotar in the air, Tom jumped with his Doolin counterpart into the air and their sticks clashed, they were off and running.

Jack spent the first ten minutes chasing shadows and gasping for air. Everything seemed to involve not just moving constantly but sprinting constantly with no breaks. Big difference to College football. When he decided to stop moving and catch his breath, a few of his teammates shouted at him to 'chase the bugger back,' or something that sounded like that.

It was not until the twentieth minute that Jack had his first touch of the sliotar. He had received a pass from Tom and the ball was now in his hand. He froze. What to do? What to do? Remembering the key message to simply smack it in the direction of the Doolin goal, he threw the ball in the air and made ready to strike. Unfortunately for him, he had taken too long, and he was about to learn that playing games without protective padding can be quite painful. Two hurling sticks clattered into him, whilst another Doolin player stuck his elbow into Jack's side. He missed the ball and the Doolin team were now in possession. More worryingly for the young American was the dig in his mid-ribs. They had winded him. He thought that he was going to vomit. This might undermine any appearance of manliness that a chap might hope to personify. Hopefully, the old guys would be standing in front of Mary and restricting her view.

He did vomit.

And he was in front of Mary.

Thankfully though the action had moved to the other side and all eyes were on the Doolin forward as he pucked the ball over the bar and between the sticks for a point.

This made Fr. Enda less than holy. He berated his defence and Robert could have sworn he heard a couple of words that he had not heard before from a Priest. The game's first half came to an end as the regulation thirty-five minutes had been played.

Robert had watched from the sidelines and was horrified by the sheer level of casual violence on display. It was as if somebody had invented a couple of rules and then called it a game. A regulated game at that, which apparently could be refereed. This was to his eyes little more than a masquerade for informal brutality. Men waving sticks at each other, not being too concerned if it hit bodies and a referee who managed to not call foul play at any point during the first half was not quite what he had expected and it has to be said, he found himself worrying for his son.

Jack had moved past the 'worry' stage. He was back in the trenches now, he just expected to be hurt, just not sure of the 'when.'

Half-time arrived, and the players were given cups of water, whilst Tom outlined the plan for the second half, they were losing 0.2 to 0.4.

Jack had only fully understood the scoring when the match was in play. If a team scored a goal that went below the bar and between the sticks, that would be worth three points. Over the bar, it was worth a point. No goals had been scored yet, so both teams had a 0, but Doolin had knocked the ball over the bar successfully four times. Lisdoonvarna only twice.

"Right lads, we have the slope for the second half. They're beginning to tire." Tom looked around at the muddied, blood-splattered faces of his team. Doolin were not the only ones who were tired.

"Micky, you, and Damo move to the forward line with Jack, and don't let that big '*hallion*' of a defender clatter into Jack again."

Michael nodded,

"And Jimmy, stop their centre. He's too good. Follow him around the pitch and if you have to....pull his shirt." He winked at Jimmy, implying that 'pulling his shirt' would be the least expected,' "Just stop him getting the sliotar."

"He's too fast," Jimmy remarked back to Tom.

"Aye, well *slow* him down, do what you have *tae*'," Tom responded and winked at him again. To make sure he understood the point.

"Okay, boys let's get back out there, and get right intae' them."

The second half progressed much the same as the first, every time a player had the ball, two, sometimes three players were clattering into them. Hurling sticks were being waved, and everybody appeared bloodied.

Jack had spent the match trying to avoid the ball and an opposition stick across the face, with Michael being highly effective at using his speed to shove players who would be moving toward Jack away. One of the Doolin's defenders had to be carried off after a particularly brutish challenge from Michael where the sliotar had left his stick a while before. The referee took him aside and told him not to tackle late again – or he would be forced to take action, next time.

Both teams had added two points each to their score and while the crowd was engrossed, the entertainment came more from the harshness of the game rather than the quality of what they were witnessing. Time was running out for Lisdoonvarna, the score was 0.4 to 0.6 in favour of Doolin, when Jack received the sliotar. He twisted away as if he was about to be blocked in American football and flicked the ball to Damo McDonagh on the wing. Jack then ran into the area a few yards in front of the goal. Damo ran past two Doolin defenders before pucking the ball to Tom, who was twenty yards from the goal. In one ballerina-like movement, he brought the ball down with his stick and when a defender was about to smash his hurling stick into Tom, Tom let fly with a rasping goal-bound shot. The Doolin goalkeeper saw it late but jumped across the goal with a flailing stick in his hand, and looked as though he would be able to push the sliotar around the post when fate intervened.

Jack had turned his back on the play but was in front of the goalkeeper. The sliotar slapped him on the back of his head and the ball looped up and over the goalkeeper's outstretched stick. Lisdoonvarna had scored. And Jack was flat on his face having been just knocked out.

His teammates were more concerned with congratulating Jack than being too worried about his well-being. They had seen this before and no doubt they would see it again.

Robert was standing beside one of the flags that represented the touchline and was now more than slightly concerned. Several minutes had elapsed, and Jack was still flat out. Tom signalled for Jonjo and a couple of the sliotar-watchers to carry Jack off the pitch. He was unceremoniously removed and dumped behind the crowd. The match had to be finished after all. Mary had a role as a partial nurse. It was partial as she had only some bandages and smelling salts. She decided to bandage the cut in the back of his head first before using the smelling salts to bring Jack around.

Robert was more than worried. His son looked a mess, yet all the attention was on the match, there were only a couple of minutes remaining.

Jack awoke sharply when Mary put the salts under his nose. He did not know where he was, other than he was looking at this most beautiful girl. His head was very sore.

"Jack, Jack," Mary shouted at him, "Can you hear me?"

The man lying down seemed to groggily nod. Then he murmured something, but Mary could not hear.

"Sorry, what did you say, Jack?"

"Where am I? Where's Mom?" It was barely a whisper, but Mary could make it out and looked up to Robert, who had not heard.

"It's okay, Jack. You've just been knocked out." Mary cradled his head in her hand.

The shouting at the match changed to a huge cheer as the referee blew for the end of the game. Lisdoonvarna had won the game by one point 1.4 to 0.6.

After shaking hands with the opposition, both teams came over to where Jack was lying. The opposition gave him a congratulatory slap of his feet or his arm as they went past. Jack's teammates were understandably more excited.

"Ya' did it Jack. Ya' did it."

"Best goal we've ever scored."

"The Yank's won it for us."

Robert Kelly was proud, worried, and perturbed. He did not understand why those around him were not more concerned about his son's injury.

"Should we not be getting him to a hospital?" He asked of Mary.

"They'll all be heading to the pubs now; it may be a struggle to get him to Limerick. It would take three to four hours. We will get him to his bed, and I will sit with him."

Jonjo O'Herlihy looked slightly askance.

"But I need you behind the bar, there'll be a thousand people wanting a pint."

Mary slapped her father down with a deathly look.

"Da' you will get six of the boys to take Jack back to the McDonagh's hotel and then and only then will they be allowed to go to the pub. He won the match, it's the least you can do."

Jonjo shook his head; his customers would not be pleased by the delay in service.

And he was afterall Mr. Service....

In fact, it was the three McDonaghs, Tim Smith, and the McGugan brothers who carried Jack back to his bed. Robert was no longer as worried as Jack was vocally telling the world how much his head was hurting. Mary had returned to the pub to find some aspirin. Jack was likely to need a couple of days' supply.

By the time she arrived at the guesthouse, everybody had scarpered to the pub. Only Robert was there with Maire attempting to feed Jack some gruel with a ladle. It was not working. Jack was becoming agitated, as was Robert.

"Och Maire, give the man some rest, here Jack, take this water and tablets," Mary propped Jack up, and gently put two tablets in his mouth, pouring a small beaker of water down his throat. She held his hand and smiled at him.

"Don't worry, nobody is going anywhere, we'll stay here until you doze off. It'll still hurt in the morning. But slightly less. And there'll still be celebratory drink during the week." She gently stroked the side of his face.

Robert struggled to contain himself, he was going to ask Mary to marry Jack on his behalf.

8

The arrival of the Dublin police that Monday morning could not have been more badly timed. The town was still recovering from an alcoholic stupor, although to be fair it was something they were well-practiced in doing and would have to deal with an influx of visitors for the festival when two police vans appeared with ten detectives in total. They had been briefed to go door to door.

Eric Nixon was with them, but he was more of a facilitator. A tall thin man, with slicked-back brown hair in his forties appeared to be in control and was giving out orders after consulting with the Ennis-based Sergeant.

Detectives spent the whole day knocking on the doors from the top of Main Street to the bottom, then down Saint Brendan's Road, before returning to Main Street and sweeping down Kincora Road.

Their inquiries were particularly slow in the morning, rather than in the afternoon. Most of the men in the houses where inquiries were being made, struggled to come down the stairs with many of the women, it has to be said also struggling. Even by the town's heroic ability to recover from a gargantuan intake of alcohol, they had, perhaps, pushed it a little far this time. Next year the match would not be arranged for the day before the start of the festival. That lesson was now learned.

The line of questioning for the police had been a little different from Sergeant Nixon's, two weeks before. Then it was just a question of going through the process as it was clear for all to see that Seamus had just dropped dead.

Yet two weeks later a report from a Dublin laboratory had told a different story.

It told of a complex arsenic that would have quickly destroyed the inside of Carville. It was a solution that could not have occurred naturally. It was a substance that had been engineered, but the laboratory could not determine where it came from.

This information aligned with oul' Dympna's comment about seeing Tom earlier that morning made the police interested. Normally it would have been handed back to Sergeant Nixon to review and decide the next steps.

But there was a small problem. Seamus Carville was known to the Dublin authorities. He was on a protected list as previously he had been a 'tout' or in more formal language an informer for the Royal Irish Constabulary in Donegal. Several individuals had been arrested and in some cases *'shot whilst trying to escape,'* but then he was found out to be a police informer.

So he was ghosted away to another part of the island, given a new identity and a new back story. He was also given a retainer to report on individuals who may have been threats to the authorities.

And he had given a few names for the police to monitor further.

Of which the name of Michael McDonagh was included on his list.

It was the senior officer who knocked on their door accompanied by Sergeant Nixon and two younger officers. Tom answered the door, it was mid-afternoon and the brothers had slept until lunchtime.

Instinctively he knew something was wrong. He could feel it, sense it, maybe it was the sullen look on Nixon's face, or the fact there were four of them just for his house.

Maire the mother felt something also, but decided not to give in to her instinct and instead went up to the Kelly's room. She needed Robert's help, could he spare her half an hour and just sit-in and listen to the policemen's conversation with her sons?

Yes, he could, and happily. Jack had been in considerable pain but was sleeping reasonably well and therefore to Robert's mind was well on the road to recovery.

He walked downstairs to join what was now a packed sitting/breakfast room.

"And who are you?" Asked the tall thin man with an unmistakable Belfast accent.

"I am Robert Kelly, sir, and Mrs McDonagh has asked me to sit in as she thinks it will also help with your inquiries."

"Does she now?"

"Yes, I do," barked the lady of the house as she marched down the wooden staircase.

"You're in my house, it will be my rules."

"And you are only making inquiries at this stage, are you not?" Kelly asked the tall thin man, before following the question up with another question, "I did not get your name?"

Eric Nixon was about to interject but the man raised his hand in a calming manner.,

"I am Chief Inspector Armstrong of the Royal Irish Constabulary, Special Branch. I will be responsible for the investigation, which you will be aware is a murder investigation," announced the man from Special Branch. He was a man who gave every impression that he expected to be listened to and obeyed. Kelly had come across this type before. He hated them. Martinets the lot of them. He tried to control his anger and kept his voice even when he responded.

"Thank you, Chief Inspector, for the record, I am a former Police detective from Philadelphia, so we are in the same unpleasant trade, I wish you well in your investigation." Kelly nodded toward Armstrong and then Nixon.

"Now, gentlemen....and ladies if we may proceed," Armstrong reasserted control and looked at Maire, "Can each of you provide any thoughts on why anybody would want to murder Seamus Carville, do you think he had any enemies? Was he engaged in any nefarious activities that you were aware of,"

"Nefarious?" Maire queried the word. She knew what it meant; it was just funny to hear it used in Lisdoonvarna.

"Sorry, I mean activities that did not seem quite right to you, they do not have to be criminal, just not right," replied Armstrong patronisingly.

"Well, he never seemed to be in the field with my boys, was he Tom? But he always had money for a drink and that house is his, he told me he bought it from work he did on the ships."

"Oh really, Mrs. McDonagh, what did he say about the ships?"

"Just that he had been on them," Maire was out of specifics, so Tom stepped in.

"He did talk about how he sailed the seas in the merchant navy, but funnily enough we never heard any stories. He talked of Calcutta and Cape Town, but he never actually described them, even when we were all ready to listen. And Ma' is right, he did some work in the fields, but only *half-baked*. Fair enough though he was older than the rest of us and he was a *blow-in*. Maybe he felt that."

"How do you mean, a 'blow-in.' pray tell?" asked Armstrong.

"Och, a blow-in? A blow-in, do you not have blow-ins in Belfast, like when all the English arrived here when they weren't invited," Michael aggressively interrupted, then smiled at his little political joke. Armstrong and Nixon's stoney faces indicated the Calvinist, Presbyterian upbringing precluded political humour.

"It's when somebody arrives from another town or area and lives beside you. Not very complicated." Tom attempted to provide a more mollified answer.

"So he was never truly accepted?"

"He has been here for a few years, I doubt anyone has a bad word to say about him, of course, he was accepted. But he kept himself to himself a lot of the time.

"Any thoughts as to why he would have been out so early in the morning?" Armstrong changed tack.

The McDonaghs looked at each other, they were all shaking their heads.

"Sometimes, we would all take a swim in the stream, and as it was warm the week Seamus passed on, maybe that was why he was up so early?"

"And why would old Dympna think that she had seen you early that morning when he died,"

"We've been through that already," Tom looked at Nixon. "She's a bit mad, she sees spirits and leprechauns,"

"But yet she was pretty sure, she saw you. Strange that." Armstrong persisted with his point. Tom simply shrugged his shoulders.

"Do you think, she could have been mistaken for either of your brothers? You know, you are the same height, same weight, and same colour of hair, do you think that could have been a possibility?"

Tom again shrugged his shoulders, Maire however did not like the direction of the 'conversation' and could contain herself no more.

"Don't you be accusin' my boys of anything, ya' hear me. You people don't rule us any longer, go back to Dublin, and take him with ya,'" She pointed at Nixon.

Once more, Armstrong raised his hand in a conciliatory manner as if testing the wind. Perhaps, with these country folk, the high hand was not the best approach.

"Nobody is being accused of anything, we are having a simple information-gathering exercise," He looked at the interloper and used him as a tool to reduce the temperature.

"Mr. Kelly, I would be correct in thinking this is standard procedure in America, you gather the information, you assess the evidence and then you consider whether to charge somebody."

"That would be correct, Inspector. Although I have noted you already arrested and then released Tom McDonagh with what could really be only described as a fig leave of justification. So I do understand why Mrs. McDonagh has a degree of cynicism."

Armstrong nodded his head, with Nixon following his lead. The two other police officers who remained standing looked on impassively.

"We acted I think a little too quickly on that one, but we corrected it, did we not?"

"I think it was Paddy Smith that corrected it, is that not more the case, Inspector?"

Armstrong merely smiled and then looked around the room,

"Well, I think that is all we need for today if you can think of anything else that may help, then we would be grateful if you could advise. I will be staying in Ennis for the next two weeks working on this case, so we may need to speak again." He then turned to Robert Kelly,

"And how long Mr. Kelly are you staying for?"

My son and I are staying until the end of the month, although we may decide to stay longer, there is no particular place we need to be." He then looked at Maire and winked,

"Unless of course, Mrs. McDonagh has had enough of us at that point." He grinned. Maire McDonagh's face lit up like a flame in the darkest night. Oh, he could stay on.

Armstrong rose and was followed out through to the narrow corridor by Nixon and the other two police officers. Tom and Maire followed them. As he left and stood outside, he turned around and remarked to Maire and Tom about what he had noticed on the wall.

"I see in addition to the large cross on the wall, you have a copy of the 1916 proclamation, do you not think that is a bit incendiary given the number of Irishmen who died because of it?"

"What business is that of yours?" Maire snapped back.

"Oh, none. Just curious." He tipped his forehead and left in the direction of the police car.

Maire McDonagh looked at her eldest and shook her head.

"They're up to something," She returned to the room with Tom behind her, shaking her head as she went. Robert Kelly had heard the comment and the exchange between Armstrong and Maire at the door.

"I think, he thinks there is something being hidden here," Kelly remarked in a sombre tone, "I'm afraid he'll be back if he does not develop any other leads, he thinks there is something in old Dympna's claims."

"Nobody was out," Maire announced in a sullen determined voice. It was as if she was speaking for the whole family, including her dead husband. Robert decided not to pursue it, yet had this been his case to investigate, he would have. They were hiding something.

The strained atmosphere was lifted with a knock at the door. It was Mary, she had returned with a small container of whiskey. Her medical knowledge was such that she knew aspirins could fix some pain and whiskey could fix other pain. She was greeted with smiles all around, particularly from Tom. Robert noted this, regretfully, but here was a girl that would attract attention, regardless of his aspirations.

Mary entered the bedroom with the small bottle of whiskey, and a jug of water with his father carrying a cup.

"And how is Mr. Head-The-Ball and believe me that is not a compliment around here," she laughed as she said it.

Jack was awake but clearly still very groggy. The bandage around his head was looking dishevelled, she requested he sat up to give her a chance to rebandage the wound. She first poured him a tumbler full, one part whiskey, three parts water, and told him only to sip it.

She put some liniment on the wound and then re-wrapped the bandage around his head.

"Doctor McHugh is coming up tomorrow from Ennis to see you, hopefully, this liniment will help, it's great for healing. You will be up and about in no time."

She really was a nurse, thought Robert Kelly. It just gets better and better.

"It's still sore," Jack muttered as he looked up and into Mary's eyes.

"Well, you can't keep lying around here, the festival is beginning today, there's a hop tonight at the Church hall and there's the walk to the *wells* tomorrow,' you'll be missing out on all the new people arriving in town. And all the girls."

Jack weakly smiled, the thought of loud music, the thought of a walk up a hill, the thought of anything right now was as far away from his thinking as it could be.

"Not sure, I will be *up* for that, Mary." He half smiled.

"Ah, sure you'll be grand in no time, now take some more whiskey." She poured him another generous helping and added the water, before turning to Robert and asking whether he would like a 'small' sip. He declined, a bit too early in the day for him.

Mary lingered a while longer, talking about nothing and everything to do with the festival with a bright smile always etched on her face. Jack was grateful for her presence, there was something motherly about her. Something that was more than just simply caring. He was going to tell her that she had been in a part of his concussed dream but thought better of it.

How could he tell her it involved a Church?

9

Brendan McManus stood leaning against the bar in O'Herlihys weighing up the rest of his day. He had a bag of products in his car that needed selling and the start of a festival with many visitors was a primary opportunity.

He had everything. Cleaning materials, paints, poultices, small hammers, screwdrivers, sharp cutting instruments, brushes, cloths, sewing materials, in short, the whole shebang.

The issue was in how to sell it without pounding up and down the streets knocking on doors. That was to be avoided at all costs, what with the weather he invariably faced most of the time.

So his experience told him, the best place to start was in the pub. He could sell some material there but also obtain intelligence on which houses may want what he had to offer. It did mean he would have to buy a couple of drinks, but he saw that as an investment. Sometimes, there would be problems when he arrived at a door, maybe a previous sale had not been quite what had been described on the tin, but Brendan always prided himself on being able to talk his way out of any situation. It was his special talent. Not one appreciated so much at school, but one that now earned him a nice living and his own place in Cork.

"That cleaning stuff of yours was powerful, we couldn't get the taste of it off our jars for a week," Gerry the barman genially remarked as he served Brendan a pint of Murphy's stout."

"Well, you knew it was clean then, I'll sell you more, where's Jonjo? There's a discount coming his way."

"I don't think Jonjo will be touching your stuff again, even with a hurling stick. Two of the customers were sick and he had to give them a night of free drink to stop them complaining."

"Well, that's never been said of my products before, I don't know what happened. Is he around? I would like the chance to make things right. I've some new stuff here, that he might be interested in trying."

"Aye, I'm sure he will," remarked a very unsure Gerry, "Anyways, he's in Ennis, not due back until later. Mary is around though, you can talk to her."

"I will at that, in the meantime, I do believe that is Turlough Bonner over there and I know his shop will need some support, excuse me, Gerry." Brendan turned and slowly wandered over to where Bonner was sitting, Gerry merely shook his head and went back to cleaning the glasses.

"Well Packy, if it isn't yourself, how have you been?"

Packy looked up at Brendan as if somebody had put a nauseous smell in the air.

"Well, since puking me' guts up for two days after taking your herbal medication, I can definitely say things have improved. You're not selling any more of that stuff, I wouldn't give it to my sheep."

"Och now, I'm sure that wasn't the case," McManus responded jovially. "It just meant you were sicker than you thought, and those medicines helped you get the bad stuff out of your body. Sure as you've just said, you were grand a few days later."

"Aye, right. I'll not be taking any more of them if it's all the same to you," Bonner cynically smiled back at Brendan. McManus nodded and maintained his smile, he had worked out there were no further business openings with this individual, so maybe best to return to the bar with his drink and sip it slowly.

He occupied his time at the bar, by taking out a small red notebook and writing in it. He kept a list of names of people who were now unapproachable. Turlough Bonnar's name had been added to that increasing list. Whilst reviewing it, Mary arrived back in. She smiled at several customers and had a word with a couple of them before heading behind the bar. Brendan made sure he caught her eye by waving his hand at her in the most unsubtle manner he could muster and then repeating her name a few times.

"Mary, Mary, Mary O'Herlihy you become more beautiful by the day. I don't know why some rascal hasn't stolen yourself away from here in a Rolls Royce."

Normally, Mary would have quipped back something about 'Awaiting such and such, to arrive with that horse-drawn carriage,' but somehow she decided against that line for McManus. He was in his thirties and his reputation had spread even to Lisdoonvarna. Also, his fluid tongue was not as attractive to her, as it was to Brendan's ears.

"Ah sure, I have a month to find my man. Starting with tonight at the Church hop. And are you going to that Brendan?"

"Sadly not, I have to return to Cork this evening. Just here to attend to business." His eyes had moved to the front door at this stage, Kevin Kearney, a local farmer had just entered the pub.

"Mary, may I be so bold as to request a couple of your finest pints of Guinness, the Murphys did not agree with me and I see my old friend, Kevin is in for some sustenance. He smiled, the smile of a man moving on to his transaction. Polite, functional, and disinterested.

Mary poured him his two pints and noted his good fortune. Their first Guinness barrel from the recent order was now empty, poor Gerry would have to go outside and wheel another one in. Nobody liked doing that job of replacing barrels, but it had to be done and as Mary never went a week without doing it at least once, she was always relieved when one of Jonjo's barmen was on duty. She wished though that it was one of her brothers instead, but quickly dismissed the idea, it caused her such melancholy.

Brendan thanked her as he lifted both glasses and plopped himself with both of them down beside Kearney.

The first hop was to be held at the Corpus Christi Hall. It was more a hut than a hall. Made entirely of wood and a cross on every upright panel. Not an obvious place from where romance could be engendered.

Priests had been drafted in from Doolin to help with the security. The presbytery had temporary beds in the sitting room to accommodate their needs. It was the busiest time of the year for the Parish Priest, Enda.

All those young men and girls meeting each other, talking with each other, dancing with each other....it all had to be managed. He never lost sight of the objective; happy Catholic marriages being created and from there strong, large, indeed very large Catholic families as the successful outcome. But it had to happen in the right way. No fraternising or God forbid, touching until both parties and most importantly the Church had judged this to be a union. Then before God, they could take their vows in holy matrimony and begin the process of breeding.

Fr. Enda always shuddered at the breeding part. He never fully understood God's plan on that one. Could he not have come up with another way, one that for instance did not involve touching and he found himself trembling when thinking about it, the bit where private parts came into contact with each other?

No, the Almighty had created a bit of a strange one with that. He preferred the stork approach. It was cleaner and involved no filth or dirt.

That was why it was important to have a brigade of priests to patrol both inside and outside the hall. These young people could become controlled by the devil. He needed his team to be aware and use their heightened senses if they suspected any improper behaviour. He knew, he knew what these young people wanted to do, and it was his duty unto God to stop it.

Six priests sat at the dining table; they were eating at 5.30 pm. Earlier than they would have done normally. Four sisters from the local convent had prepared an Irish stew and were now reheating the meal in the biggest of brass pots. They would eat after the holy men of the Lord. As they too were in the protection vanguard. All those girls needed the armour that the nuns could offer. Never trust boys, but always trust priests.

Sister Joan never liked the festival. It took her away from prayer and contemplation. That was the life she signed up for. Feeding priests was one thing, but engaging with the world and stopping the basest of base human instincts was quite another. When the festival was over she would hide herself away and focus on the rosary. She would think of Mary and what she had gone through as a mother and a woman. The month-long festival was Sister Joan's penance, she would offer it up to Mary. One woman's offering to another. She too had been selected for a task she had not asked for, but she would carry it out with love. Or whatever could enable her to survive the month.

The briefings had taken place to the religious and they were advised on what to look out for and to be weary of Willie O'Neil. He was the matchmaker, the *Seachtair*. He would be hovering around encouraging conversations and frankly to Fr Enda's mind, encouraging sin. They need to keep an eye on the young people and an eye on him as well.

Willie O'Neil was sitting at the bar with his notebook out in front of him. He was due to be visited by one of the Dolan sisters, Sinead. She had her eyes on a particular boy and wanted his guidance on how best to make him interested in a match. For Willie, this was his speciality. The girls were always keener on finding true love, with the boys they tended to be practical, and everything had to be presented to them as a practical solution then they were off on love's journey. Obviously, it required supervision, not the Church's version of course. That was too restrictive, it did not allow for love to blossom in all its beautiful meandering forms.

That's why the matchmaker's role was so important. He knew, he just knew. It was a gift he had inherited from his father, a gift aligned with ruthless administration (names, ages, types of all the boys and girls) that enabled him to move the pieces around the love chessboard. For this reason, he had a certain respect for 'oul Dympna. She also knew, instinctively on other facets of life. The main difference between the two of them being, she was in his view, quite mad.

Mary was going round to Siobhán's to make herself ready for the dance. The Dolan sisters would also be there. Sinead, Deirdre, and Breda. They were good fun. Each one of them with hair redder than the other. They made Siobhán look blonde in comparison. They would call in on the McDonaghs ostensibly to see Jack before the hop began.

Siobhán had a wee eye on Damian and Mary, well she did like Tom a bit more than he knew, but how could she not take a shine to Jack? Then there was Tim.

She knew that Jack's dad liked her anyway, so that was a useful start.

The girls put on their new stockings. This was always a treat, and they applied each other's lipstick and eye shadow. It was a ritual and unlike every other month of the year, there was a chance of something happening that would be life-changing. Any of the other dances that may have taken place during the year invariably saw all the boys taking too much drink.

That was off-putting, particularly when as a girl you realised that the talent pool was already thin enough on the ground.

But there was always something about the festival, the boys behaved themselves and kept their drinking to a minimum. Some of them would even attempt to dance properly, they were never much good, even though they tried. It helped create a romantic air, a mood of joy, dare one say it even, love.

At any rate, that's what the girls hoped for.

The hop was due to begin at 8 pm and finish at 10.45 pm, so the plan was to be ready by just after 7, nip across and say hello to Jack, and of course, let all the McDonagh boys see how good they looked, then proceed to the hall.

It was five past eight before they left the house. Blame was being apportioned for this reason and that. An unpleasant edge had entered the sisterhood. The Dolans wanted to go straight to the hall as they were 'pretty certain' the McDonaghs would be already there, and others would be *hovering* around them.

Nonetheless, Mary, because she was the oldest bullied them across the road and they knocked on the door.

Maire answered it.

She looked deeply, deeply unimpressed by what she saw. It would never have happened in her day and her boys needed to be very careful with these *wee* madams. The boys thankfully for Mary had not left yet, but with the noise of giggling girls at the door, they bounced to their feet and within seconds had brushed their mother aside to show off their freshly washed shirts.

Mary and Siobhán were allowed to go upstairs.

Jack was sitting up in bed, whilst his dad was in an armchair reading a rather large awkward-looking book. Small, but very fat.

He greeted them with a smile, as did Jack.

"And how's the town's hero?" Mary asked breezily.

"Sore and now that I have been awake for a couple of hours, a bit bored."

"Read a book, then," his father unhelpfully suggested.

"Och now, Mr. Kelly, I'm sure Jack is in no fit state to read. When the Doctor comes tomorrow that'll make it all better."

"Yeah," Jack muttered doubtfully.

"People always are hit with sliotar at these matches, yes maybe you were hit a bit harder than most, but it always clears up in a few days. And at least you've been able to stay in bed, all the others who have been, always have to go back to the fields. Nobody looks after them. They just have to get on with it."

"Exactly Mary, exactly." Robert rejoined in support.

Jack listened to the 'Get on with it,' comment and was going to retort, 'Will try the trenches then,' but decided against it. He did not need this subject to continue.

"So you are both going to the hop then?"

"That, we are," Siobhán responded and then proceeded to twirl her dress. Robert Kelly applauded. Mary decided not to follow suit and instead laughed as Siobhán enjoyed all the eyes on her.

"What time is this Doctor coming tomorrow."

"Early afternoon, he may come early because of the festival. He'll be a busy man, I'm sure, but he knows about your injury. Tim Smith has informed him."

"Is Tim at the hop tonight?"

"Probably," a guarded Mary answered.

"He would make someone a good husband, would he not?" Jack teased.

"Probably," Mary responded again and then followed it up, "Are you thinking of marrying him yourself, there Jack?"

"Ho, ho, you are so funny," Jack rolled his eyes.

"That's from working at the bar, you learn quick." Mary smiled and looked at Siobhán,

"Right let's be joining the Dolans and dancing ourselves into a tizzy."

They both kissed Jack gently on his bandaged head and made their way downstairs.

Siobhán was a little angry that Sinead, Breda and the McDonagh twins had already left for the hall. Tom had remained with Deirdre to walk the girls there. A gentleman.

Yet, with his mother shouting for him, 'to be careful' it was not a ringing endorsement of his independence.

10

The dancing was in full swing by the time Tom, Mary, Deirdre, and Siobhán arrived.

Tim Smith was surrounded by the remaining Dolan sisters and evidently enjoying every single minute of it. Sister Joan less so, she was hovering around with Fr. Enda like a shark looking for its prey, fin out of the water moving diagonally amongst the shoals of fish. Early action had been taken by the junior priests as one of the dances, '*When you look in the heart of a rose*,' had caused early carnage with younger, less experienced males holding their girl for just a bit too long.

The steady arm of the morality police had then stepped in and forced 'the individual to leave the field of play.' And this appeared to be happening quite often as the number of dances that had only the girls doing the dancing had started to increase. For this reason, the Marian Harms classic, '*A good man is hard to find*,' received two airings in one segment.

The band itself was '*Big P and the Baseliners*,' they were so called as the lead singer was Padraig, he was over six foot and a little overweight with glasses that seemed huge on him despite his size. The Baseliner element came from the favoured choice of instruments, which included a double bass, a cello, and two fiddlers, who were being qualified as bass for the purposes of the name.

Padraig had considered other naming options, but with a heavy heart had decided, that *Big P and the Fiddlers* would not probably cut it with obtaining bookings and may leave him open to other interpretations. So, he used his instrument genre instead.

The 1920s West of Ireland music scene could be merciless.

Their musical scope was limited but growing and focused on covers of any popular John McCormack number as he was from just up the road in Athlone, one hundred miles away, local enough. But there was also a smattering of newer jazzy numbers from across the Atlantic that were now becoming popular in the Dublin city music halls that Big P thought useful to add to the repertoire. He believed firmly in constantly updating the band's musical inventory, regardless of whether they had the right instruments or in his case, the right voice.

By and large, it worked, wherever they went, they always had good crowds who seemed to enjoy themselves and they were rarely not invited back. There was only that disaster in Shannon that blotted the copybook, but how could he be blamed if his previous fiddler had been caught '*in flagrante delicto*' with the local Church of Ireland Minister's daughter? You really cannot expect a thirty-one-year-old daughter of the manse to be so uninhibited. Still, he had learned his lesson, and that fiddler was replaced.

The first interval arrived, and Big Tom's ensemble took a well-earned break. Jonjo O'Herlihy was running the temporary bar with one of his barmen. There was not going to be much trade anyway at his own bar as all the young, youngish, not so youngish but single people would be at the hop. The older single mainly men, well actually they would all be men, who were in the pub could wait. They would be nursing their pints anyway, so Charlie could look after them. Gerry was better for this crowd. He had recently become a father for a third occasion and welcomed any time he could spend out of the house. Any time at all.

It also has to be said that Jonjo himself had an agenda. He wanted to keep his eye on Mary. She was the most precious thing in his life. And although she had stopped listening to him a while ago and his influence over her was somewhere between oblivion and zero, she was still his.

Of the prospects in the town, there were only two that could pass muster. He was not desperately keen on either. Tim Smith, Paddy's son would probably take over the father's legal practice once he had completed his exams, exams he had been taking for several years apparently, so already there was a query on his diligence and that was leaving aside, his regular time to study at Dublin University with all the question marks around his behaviour there. Rumours did travel and the rumours with Tim were that of a lady's man. So not suitable for his Mary.

Then there was Tom. Solid, dependable, reliable Tom. With the daft mother who he suspected had designs on him, as they were widowed.

No, Tom would be a complication for Jonjo. The Christmas Days would no doubt become something he would begin to dread. The baptisms, the church engagements, the big happy family times that would mean, constant exposure to Maire. All very difficult.

So it was with regret that Jonjo was concluding that his Mary would have to find someone from beyond Lisdoonvarna. She would have to leave. For her own good. And that would break his heart.

His role until then was to make sure it was for the right chap.

That young American boy could be the ticket, except, of course, Mary would have to leave Ireland. Going to Dublin was one thing, but across the Atlantic was another.

At any rate, he would focus on who would go after her tonight and indeed who she went after. He would have to protect her from herself.

And this West of Ireland 1920's dad, who when it came to his daughter lived in the 1820's with regard to her virtue, was the only father who could enforce it. Properly.

With Big P and the Baseliners break over, the music started up again with a few of the more modern songs taken from the music hall and the latest gramophone recordings.

It would be fair to say that the Baseliners could probably have done with a bit more practice on a few of them, well all of them, but the crowd really did not care. They were there to meet the opposite sex.

The amount of smoke in the room made it difficult to see the band from the back, for this reason, all the Priests with their Commander-in-Chief, Fr. Enda, accompanied by the Nun squadron led by Sister Joan had to weave their way around, and following some sort of tactical discussion at the interval had decided the boys needed to be encouraged to put their pints down and ask the girls to dance. There was increasing concern that drunk males would not make for attractive catches. Fr. Enda had already requested that Jonjo water down the drink a bit more. Something Jonjo was always happy to facilitate. Had it been his regulars, they would have burned the place to the ground.

So with the tempo of the music having increased and big Tom moving into his John McCormack set, beginning with 'Love, here is my heart,' Tim grabbed Mary's hand for a dance. Initially, she displayed reluctance before sighing in the direction of Siobhán and accepting the request. Not that Siobhán was looking back, she was up dancing with Damian and enjoying every single second of it. Until Sister Joan came in and placed a ruler between them. They had been too close. The umpire had made a decision. Siobhán rolled her eyes at Damian, whilst he winked back and despite the distance between them having been adjusted to acceptable standards, they found themselves gripping each other's forearms more tightly. Try stopping that one, Sister, became the non-verbal communication as their eyes met and smiles widened.

Mary was secretly enjoying the dance with Tim; she knew what her father knew. The choices were limited, and this was one of the choices. She also knew his reputation. They fox-trotted, something he proved to be very good at and they shouted a conversation of sorts at each other.

"You should come for a spin in the car with me again, we can go down to Limerick. Or up to Galway. Or if you like, down to Cork."

"Ooh, that's too far."

"We could stay the night, separate rooms of course,"

Mary eyed him with the 'I know what you are doing Tim Smith' look but was again secretly pleased he was at least making a semblance of an effort. After a couple of dances, where Big P and the band would have been convicted of murder had John McCormack heard their renditions, he invited her outside to continue the conversation. She smiled, then laughed before politely refusing using the time-honoured excuse of 'needing to find her friend,' Tim had made his play and it had not been rebuffed. He would now return to dance with one of the Dolan sisters suspecting that Mary would keep a mindful eye on his progress.

Mary did want to find Siobhán. She saw her as a younger sister, but with the combination of smoke, sweaty bodies, and the morality police, she could not find her. Briefly, she became worried, so she went to the temporary bar and shouted over to her dad whether he had seen her. He had. She had left a few minutes earlier to go outside and have a cigarette with 'young McDonagh.' Jonjo had raised his eyebrow at Mary with condemnatory judgment written all over it. Mary shrugged and half smiled before making her way to the door. She bumped into Tom, who it appeared was also looking for someone, his younger brother Damian.....

They both stepped outside and found themselves looking at five couples who appeared as though they were being lined up for execution.

Fr. Enda and Sister Joan were laying into them for sneaking off and as two of them had been caught kissing, there was a sermon to be given to all on where this might lead to, with the fires of hell being described dramatically by the two religious people.

"Touching is wrong, do you hear me? Wrong. That's for marriage and only holy, holy marriage. When you have taken vows in front of God himself. Only then. This low, vile, and Godless behaviour is the devil himself, who is talking to you. You hear me? The devil himself." Fr. Enda breathed with fire coming from his nostrils. Sister Joan thought it was important for the feminist in her to show itself. Although it was not the feminism that could be seen in efforts to win the vote or take control of their money, this was an older form, apparently.

"And you girls, you girls, and your wickedness. Do not trust these boys. I know what they're after, even if you don't." Which of course was not strictly true, the convent she had been educated in, talked of the birds and bees without doing the actual biology. She was not entirely sure herself about the specifics, however, what was abundantly clear to her was that it was all wrong.

Wrong. Wrong. Wrong. And those girls needed to know that.

Mary and Tom looked at the sheepish expressions on Siobhán and Damian's faces. They enjoyed the young people's embarrassment.

"Maybe now that we know they are fine, we should return inside," Tom suggested to Mary. Mary nodded whilst still laughing at what she had witnessed.

Willie O'Neil had taken out his notebook, he had noted the couplings, and there would be individual visits later made by him to determine whether these prospective partnerships would require his unique oversight.

Mary had returned to the hall and had expected Tom to ask her for a dance, but he did not. He seemed to shy away from doing so, but then that was Tom. Quiet, reliable, and at times incredibly shy, Tom. Mary was going to let it go but then noted Tim Smith appeared to be dancing with two girls at the same time. His perfect movement and effervescence suggested both confidence and enjoyment. He knew he was a catch if not 'the' catch. So Mary thought to herself, two could play that game. She grabbed Tom and walked him to the dance floor. Big P was at this point moving toward their grand finale, the band's musical repertoire was not made for four hours of different material. So the newest had to be kept for the end and his newest was a couple of songs from the Ziegfeld Follies, which Padraig had seen at the Gaiety Theatre in Dublin when the cast was on a short tour of Europe.

He loved the music and could see the future; the trouble was you needed more than what he had to give it, its true effect. But Big P was nothing if not a trier, or a chancer depending on who you talked to, and he had the band practising a version of what he remembered. So they began with '*A pretty girl is like a melody*,' with Big P hitting the high notes that Robert Steel would hit with ease, in a manner that indicated he needed more scaffolding. Much, much more. The crowd did not care.

Tom was clumsy, his two clod-hopping feet could not move in time with anything least of all the music. Mary who had spent hours and hours practising the dances with her friends attempted to guide him, but the more she thought she was helping the worse Tom became. He was at a level of pain that no whack from a hurling ball – and that included the one Jack took – could be anywhere near as traumatic. This was not his world.

Mary recognised Tom's discomfort but felt he needed to push through his pain and shyness barrier. She also wanted Tim Smith to see her having fun. However, she began to realise that what Tom was experiencing was a form of death. He never complained, because the big, wonderful, reliable, lump never did. When the four-minute song had ended in what was for Tom the longest four minutes of his life, Mary pulled his arm and took him off the dance floor.

"Sorry, sorry, sorry, Tom. Siobhán and I are going to give you lessons on your footwork. By the next hop, you will be the best dancer of the lot." She said it jovially in the hope, that Tom would respond to her brightness. He did not.

"I'm not sure this is for me Mary, it's not a hurling field." He sighed, defeated.

"Nonsense, everybody can dance. You just need to give it a go."

Tom looked at her and smiled. He felt unworthy of her, she was beautiful, nice, and funny. He was just not like her. She could make people laugh, was comfortable with everybody and in every situation. He was not. He could never make himself a good enough husband for her, no matter how hard he wished it.

"Tim's a right good dancer," He smiled at Mary and stated the obvious as the garrulous solicitor's son danced towards them.

"Ah, sure his daddy will have paid for the lessons, and he was able to practice when he was away," Tom nodded as Mary inadvertently identified the chief characteristics that enabled Tim to be the better prospective husband. Perhaps it was the look on Tom's face, was it disappointment? But Mary realised that was the wrong comment at the wrong time to the wrong person, she attempted to tidy things up, suspecting that it may also make things worse.

"Well, he's not as strong as you and you're a much better hurler." Tom smiled. Politely. They both knew embarrassed false flattery when they heard it.

Big P had just finished his rendition of '*I love a piano,*' when the fiddler struck up a chord for the next massacre, '*Alexander's Ragtime Band.*'

Tim Smith grabbed Mary's wrist from behind and pulled her onto the dance floor. Tom's evening was now complete. She was caught unawares and laughed before stopping herself and looking back towards Tom.

But at that point, he had gone.

11

Jack had woken in a sweat. It felt like it was the middle of the night given the amount of snoring that was coming from his dad's bed. His head was sore again but in a different way. The pillow was wet, he was oozing something and although not a medical expert, he knew this could not be good. Strangely he felt well enough to rise from his bed and found himself steadier on his feet than he thought he would. The concussion was wearing off, he reasoned.

He used the wall to help with balance, just in case, and carefully opened the door. The big grandfather clock indicated it was 6.15 am. Gingerly he made his way downstairs. The floorboards creaked to the point that Jack thought not only would the house be awoken, but the whole town as well.

He made his way into what could be nominally described as the kitchen. In the middle of the table was a bucket with water in it. He took the ladle beside it and poured some water into a cup and sipped tentatively, touching his head as he did so. His head felt on fire, and he was desperate to pour some water onto the head gash. He unwound the bandage and took off the linen dressing Mary had used for his head. He looked at the blood on the linen and what he thought was pus-like fluid. This was definitely not good. The injury was going septic. He opened the back door to the yard and walked to the outdoor toilet with the bucket of water. Once there he opened the half door and put his head over the hole and then using the ladle proceeded to lift water and trickle it over the wound.

He knew enough to know the need to clean the open gash. Something with Mary's nursing had gone very wrong here.

He emptied the bucket and as well as his head being soaking, so were his pyjamas. There was nothing to dry himself off with, so dripping with water he returned to the kitchen with the bucket.

Maire McDonagh was up.

"What are you doing out of bed....in your condition, as well? Jesus, Mary, and Joseph, what is wrong wid' you?'"

"Well, Mrs. McDonagh, my head was oozing."

"Oozing? Oozing? Let me see." She peered down at the wound which had stopped bleeding but was now forming a vaguely yellow fluid around it.

"That's not right, that's not right a t'all," she said, shortening her 'at' and adding an extra letter to her 'all.'

"What time is Dr. McHugh coming today?" She asked of Jack.

"I'm not entirely sure, Mary seemed to think it would be in the afternoon,"

"Well, we'll need to see about that, something not right here a t'all. Not right a t'all. I'll send Michael to take the cart over to Kilfenora, as that's where he always goes to first before coming up here, and tell the Doctor to come straight over."

"Do you think it's that serious?" Jack queried with both concern and surprise in his voice.

"It's serious enough for me, to bring you back out to the yard now and pour more cold water over it." She grabbed his arm and virtually pulled him outside. If there was one thing she knew, it was the healing effects of the water, sure the wells around here were mystical after all.

Oul' Dympna knew, and Maire had seen it for herself over the years when 'fixing' the grazes that her boys would come home with.

"Och, you'll be fine now for a while, the doctor will be able to do the rest."

Jack noted the different nursing styles of Maire and Mary, one was caring and tender, the other brutish and sure-footed. He knew which one was preferred....and yet, that one may have caused a problem, rather than help resolve it. After Maire drenched his head again, she patted it down with a clean towel and then defaulted to the final aspect of the healing process, that was used in every Irish medical prescription.

"Now, I'll make you a nice cup of tea and you'll feel much better." She said with a big smile, once she had uttered the word 'tea.'

"Er, yeah sure." Jack looked at her, he was not so certain now that leaving the room and his father's snoring was the best thing to do. He was hoping one if not all the boys would be up from bed. The thought of a one-on-one with Maire for the next hour was going to be tough.

He was in luck.

Michael was up, he had heard the floorboards creaking and found himself caught short. He had only returned from the hop a few hours earlier. So his sleep had been light and when he heard the creaking, his efforts to fall asleep again by tossing and turning had yielded nothing. So he arose and went downstairs. He moved at pace, past his mother and Jack into the kitchen and then out to the yard.

The only thing he knew was that his mother would have a cup of tea ready for him when he returned.

"And when the doctor comes," Maire began for the fourth time, "Make sure you tell him about the water, it will have reduced the swelling, sure look I can see it getting smaller from here." She had decided against re-applying the bandage, she just knew this type of thing needed 'air.' All this nonsense from young people who think they know how to fix things.... 'Water, air, and time,' was all that was ever needed.

It was midday before Dr. McHugh arrived to see Jack. By this point, Mary had been over, ostensibly to check on his well-being and tell him all about the hop. However, maybe there was another motive for Mary, to check in on Tom. But he was already out in the fields.

"And sure, there was a lot of handholding with that Deirdre Dolan dancing with literally all the boys. She did not miss one of them. She's such fun."

Jack listened politely, Michael had already provided a debrief, which was short, sharp, and to the point. Key facts only in description. Mary on the other hand went around the houses, speculating on who was thinking what, and what their real plan was. Beginning every sentence with either; "Och, sure," or "Aye, sure." She at no point paused for questions. Which were unlikely to come anyway. She was completely immersed in her retelling of the evening. Then Siobhán joined her.

This gave the story a new wind, with new angles to be explored and as her romance with Damian was now confirmed, she felt the need to call in, ostensibly of course to see Jack, but secretly it was Damian she wanted the first morning look at.

Jack for her as a possible contender was now well and truly banished from her mind. She had her sights set and like a marksman lining up her target, she felled him. It was now a case of making sure he remained 'felled.'

Willie O'Neil would be receiving a visit later.

So by the time, Dr. McHugh had arrived, Jack had a splitting head caused by more than the smack of a sliotar ball.

McHugh looked at the skull and seemed to spend the time murmuring to himself, "This won't do, this won't do."

"Now Jack, *wouldcha*' be telling me who dressed your wound and what liniment they used?"

Robert Kelly attempted to answer for his son, he had exited stage left when Siobhán had arrived as whilst he had just been about able to listen to Mary drivel on, the thought of new wind and fresh energy for the subject matter was just too much. He loved his son, but there were limits and this was one bullet Jack needed to take himself. When the doctor arrived, however, Robert was able to use this opportunity to close down the schoolgirl talking shop with the gravity only a senior detective from the Philadelphia police could bring. Or at least that was what he told himself.

Dr. McHugh was a man who was looking down the barrel of his seventieth year. He loved his job, and he loved where he lived. These were his people. The good, the bad, and those with two teeth.... as he frequently remarked. He wore a three-piece tweed suit that was made timeless by his waistcoat watch chain. His small horn-rimmed glasses seemed to Robert to possibly be for effect as he never seemed to look through them. Whenever Dr. McHugh talked to you, his eyes met yours above them and Robert noted when he examined Jack's head wound, that he did not use them either. Even when he arrived in his car, he seemed not to be using them. At any rate, the doctor looked at the wound for several minutes, before asking the question on the source of nursing care.

"Young Mary, Jonjo's daughter from O'Herlihys did the nursing and I have to say I thought she did an exceptional job," He would defend Mary's corner from the challenge he felt was about to arrive.

"Did she now?" McHugh wrote the comment down in his little pocketbook. Then went unnervingly silent for a few minutes, before clearing his throat. Then returning to silence. Jack looked at his father. His father looked back at his son. All a bit strange. Then finally, the good doctor from Ennis spoke.

"Well Jack, your wound has become infected, but it's an infection, I see mostly after gunshots. And I see too many of them," He remarked sternly. "Whatever that girl used was actually poisonous to your wound, but I see Maire has poured the waters over it and that will help. I am also going to ask her to find some honey, I want it applied in the morning and again in the evening. That will clear out the infection within a week. But there is a chance you may run a fever for a while, it's difficult to know. If you do, take plenty of water. That will make you better, quick enough." He smiled benignly, his summary for the patient was complete.

"I need to speak to that Mary girl, she should not be using what she's using," He said while putting away his notebook and stethoscope.

"Thank you, Doctor," Robert again took the lead, "I'm sure Mary will have had a good reason to use the liniment she used."

"She may have a good reason, but it is a wrong reason. This is not a question of opinion; this is a question of fact.

Now if you'll excuse me, I have others to see. I will give this note on the honey to Maire, and she'll find some from somewhere and do the dressing for you for the whole week."

Oh God, thought Jack. Oh God, thought Robert. It was going to be a long week.

12

Jonjo O'Herlihy had spent the Tuesday morning in bed. The hop had finished at 10.30 pm, but he had not finished packing up the mobile bar with Gerry until nearly 1 am. He then had his time taken up further with an enforced drink with the Priests at the presbytery, which of course he had to supply *gratis*. The Nuns had returned to the convent in a two-horse pony and trap driven by Sister Joan. That represented a saving, at least that was how he saw it, particularly when Fr. Enda took out the whiskey bottle from the crate and poured a generous helping for each of the Priests as a reward for a 'job well done.'

Sin had been in the air, but it was vanquished and they, the vanguard of 'good' had overseen, good Catholic boys and girls, begin the first faltering steps on the journey to family life.

Jonjo wanted his bed, but he was currently being baked into what was becoming an impromptu 'backslapping, we're against the devil' session. He needed to take decisive action.

"Now gentlemen, I have a business to run, but feel we should round off the evening with another wee drink and toast the Corpus Christi Church for its fine work in bringing people together." This time he picked up the bottle and added to each of the priest's glasses with a much smaller tipple than Fr. Enda's measure. He nodded to Gerry, who was standing.

"May the Lord continue to bless our town and the festival, what a great start, Sláinte!" He raised his voice with his glass for the final word. It was repeated back to him by all the clerics. He then proceeded to grab the crate of whiskey, whilst Gerry grabbed the other and marched out of the front door in the direction of his pub. The empty glasses and cups could be cleaned up tomorrow. This was about maintaining profitability.

Mary was still up when he returned, she was rinsing the glasses of the few regulars who instead of going to the hop had baked themselves into the pub for the evening. She also was still buzzing. Adrenalin coursed through her veins. Her core group of girls had returned to the pub as it was after closing time and they had distilled the key takes from the evening. Siobhán was going to marry Damian, Breda Dolan was going to marry Michael and Mary was set-up for life with Tim. They giggled and laughed as plans were made as to which of the remaining Dolan girls would marry Tom. Maybe they both would, surely the Catholic Church would allow that marriage if it involved two *good* Cath-.., well, two Catholic girls anyway?

The girls had returned to their homes to smother their pillows and dream, dreams that they would tell their mothers in the morning. And those same mothers would smile back, be excited for them, and then inwardly sigh. They too had had the same dreams, life however proved not to be so simple.

"I saw you dancing with Tom and Tim, " Jonjo smirked toward his daughter.

"I did at that, I'm happy you were keeping your eye on me," Mary returned the cynical smile.

"Do you have a fancy for one of them?" He queried.

"I probably fancy them both, but yet, yet not enough."

Jonjo nodded, he did not know how to have these conversations, it would be different had Emer still been alive. She would have known how to guide. He could not make up his mind on what was the most suitable option for his daughter. However, in fairness, he also understood that even if he did have a clear view, she would quickly sniff out if he was nudging her in a particular direction.

"Maybe go see Tom, tomorrow. I'm not sure these hops are his world. He is a good boy."

Mary smiled knowingly at her father.

"I had planned to; I know he is." She returned to the bucket that was full of glasses, rinsing the soap off them individually.

"Do we have enough powder?" Jonjo asked changing the subject.

"We are running out,"

"I will do a run to Ennis in the morning and pick up some more, maybe if you have time make a list with Charlie on what we need to cover the rest of the month. I don't want to be relying on Brendan's overpriced rubbish if I can avoid it."

"Yessir," shouted Mary back to her dad and then saluted him for good measure.

"Don't be cheeky my girl, don't be cheeky," he turned around and headed upstairs to his bed. She would be quite the catch for a chap, that one.

And he would be lost without her. Utterly, utterly lost.

13

By Friday, Jack's swelling had reduced considerably, and the yellow fluid was rapidly disappearing. Maire had been able to source honey from her cousin who lived in Lahinch with Damian travelling a round-trip of three hours to pick it up. She knew how to look after her guests. Or at least those with a bad head injury.

Jack felt well enough to request that his dad put his 'damn book down' and take him to O'Herlihys for a lunchtime drink. He was going insane and wanted to see the preparations for the weekend as this would be the first big weekend of the festival.

His father was reading Hamlet......Sigh.

They entered the pub with Robert being greeted with a nod from the several regulars with whom he would have a drink every day. He did not see any point in both of them suffering because of Jack's misfortune. Mary saw Jack and lit up with a smile.

"It's great to see you out of bed," she announced before taking off her apron and coming round the side of the bar to hug him. She then looked at Charlie behind the bar and placed the order.

"I think these two fine men, would be needing a couple of pints. They're on the house, but don't be tellin' Da," This provoked a smile from Jack and a laugh from Robert. She pulled them over to the corner table, whilst Charlie brought their drinks over.

"How are you feeling, Jack?"

"Better. Much better. Just completely bored. Dr. McHugh is banning everybody except Maire from touching me." He rolled his eyes, "But at least, I had Dad here as company, oh wait that's right, you spent your time reading when you were not coming down here for a pint and a chat." He looked sternly at his father. Mary looked at him slightly bemused.

"Your Dad's only been in quickly every day, he hasn't stayed." Robert began to shift uncomfortably.

"Er, son, I've been on a horse for the last few days. I didn't want to tell you, but I'll be riding in the Lisdoonvarna Festival four-miler tomorrow."

"Whaaaat?"

"I meant to tell you, son," He looked up apologetically, "Bob McFarlane suggested it last week and what with your injury and all, I didn't think it would help your recovery."

Jack laughed out loud.

"It would have, and if you fall from the horse, I am going to insist you have two weeks of one-to-one with Maire. Then let's see who gets married first." He laughed again at the very thought. Mary half joined in. There was something in the word 'marriage' with Jack's hint of disdain that she found off-putting.

"When was the last time you were on a horse Dad?"

"As you know very well, I grew up with horses, son. Your grandad's first job was on the farms before we went to the city when I was twelve. I didn't just spend my time milking the cows." It was now Robert's turn to look sternly at Jack, had he never listened to him talking about his past? Mary could sense a slight edge between father and son, so redirected the conversation slightly,

"So which horse has Bob given you?"

"Whiskey in the Jar."

"That's a bit of a mouthful, Dad."

"It is, but easy to remember. After this pint, I will introduce you to him."

"The Lisdoonvarna ride is always a lot of fun, it used to be the boys would have to grab the bonnet of the girl they loved. So romantic. It's changed a bit now," Mary said mournfully.

"I'll ask Maire for one of her hats, no reason why we cannot see the tradition started again, eh, Dad? That would be really lovely. And very, very funny."

Except Robert was not finding it so funny and grimaced. "Not amusing son, not amusing."

"I think the knock on your son's head hasn't fully healed, by the sound of that attitude...." Mary was taking the dad's side. Strategically a good move, but she was a bit annoyed with Jack. Maire may have been hard work, but she was a good woman and why would she not be someone that could find romance later in her life?

"So where is your Dad, Mary?" Robert asked.

"Oh, he's away to Ennis buying stock, it's been a good week," she smiled ruefully. "And he'll be stocking up on liniment and gauze. We'll not be buying any of Brendan's stuff again. Sorry about that."

"Oh don't worry Mary. It's getting better now." Jack touched his head and smiled.

The Kellys finished their drinks and made their way to McFarlane's farm intent on visiting 'Whiskey in the Jar' but found their attention diverted by a commotion down the street. Close to where their lodgings were. They walked towards the disturbance; it was outside their Hotel. Sergeant Nixon was there with several police officers. Maire was in uproar and Tom was being held back by the policemen. As they approached they saw Michael, one of the twins being led out of the front door in handcuffs before being lifted into the back of a police wagon.

A small crowd had formed made up of locals and several tourists who were there for the festival. They were shouting abuse at the police. Inspector Armstrong came out of the house and spoke to Nixon, before making his way to a waiting car with two policemen. He was barracked the whole way.

Robert Kelly caught his eye, he stopped and walked toward him.

"Mr. Kelly out of professional courtesy, I will tell you what I have told Michael McDonagh, his mother, and family. We have received further information that the victim's background, was known to Michael McDonagh. This information comes on top of an identification of Mr. McDonagh being seen close to the dead man at the time of his death. Therefore we are duty-bound to act. He has been arrested because we suspect him of murder. He is not a witness and will be questioned as an accused man. We have informed his solicitor." Armstrong nodded to Kelly and then went directly to the car.

Tom had been released from the lock the police had on him and he was now holding his mother as she cried into his arms. Damian was standing beside them shaking his head.

"They hate us, they hate us....." Maire kept repeating.

"Paddy Smith will get him out, he got me out, he'll get Micky out," Tom tried to reassure her, but it was not working. She continued to sob.

The police wagon departed with Armstrong's car, leaving Nixon with the remaining two policemen. A rock was thrown at them, then several more. They retreated towards their car but had their way blocked, by a growing mob of fifteen people.

"Stand away, please. We are doing our job."

The crowd did not stand away, more stones were thrown from behind that hit the crowd as much as the police.

Robert and Jack stood back as they were not sure what to do. Then a voice cut through the air, Maire was speaking,

"Leave them be, Leave them be," she shouted, and then looking at Sergeant, she remarked for all to hear, "I might not like you Eric Nixon, but you're not a bad man. My son is innocent, go protect him from that detective."

The crowd began to disperse slowly, and the policemen made their way to the car, Robert followed them quickly to the car.

"Sergeant Nixon, this is not my business but if they are using oul' Dympna, as with Tom, this will not work in court."

"There is a new witness, Mr. Kelly." Came the curt reply, but how Nixon looked at Kelly as he said it indicated, that the Sergeant was less than convinced.

"I would request that you support Maire, we will do our jobs in Ennis without fear or favour and if the evidence threshold is not met, Michael will be released. You have my word on that and please tell Maire that, as well."

Robert nodded. Nixon had just communicated with him that he was not comfortable with the arrest. Something else was afoot.

14

Paddy Smith had been advised by Eric Nixon before they had departed from Ennis to make the arrest that he should keep the afternoon free. Armstrong had been against this idea but could not overrule Nixon.

Michael McDonagh had been taken to Ennis police station, protesting his innocence the whole way, but nobody was listening.

He was in the cell by himself for an hour before Paddy Smith arrived. Much to McDonagh's surprise, his solicitor seemed to be taking a rather avuncular approach,

"Well, well, well, another week and another McDonagh, now what is it with your family? I'm surprised your mother hasn't arrived to burn this place down," he laughed as if he was imagining the scene.

"So I have talked to Sergeant Nixon and understand the basis of their evidence, it's probably enough to get you to a court, and if the jury is handpicked by people from Belfast then you'll be found guilty."

"Why would that matter?" Michael queried.

"Because you are a young fool, aren't you Michael?"

"No, I'm not." Michael was beginning to wonder about this 'help.'

"Well now, it seems they know you have been on the fringes of the IRA; you've attended meetings and their late evening and early morning drills on the hillsides. And it's probably from one of those that you walked past poor

Seamus's body when you were returning. Isn't that likely to be the case?"

Michael began to look sheepish.

"Now their issue is going to be where did you obtain the poison from, and they will have a huge problem with that, so they may simply rely on saying you received it from so-and-so, whoever it is they wish to charge next, and say you simply followed an order to kill Seamus."

"But why would I have wanted tae' kill him?"

Smith looked at this young man, who was barely twenty. A young fool, who was no more capable of committing a murder as he was of flying to the moon.

"Seamus had been a minor informer, Michael. There are people who will be glad that he is dead. And that's why we have a problem. So what you are going to do is everything I tell you to do. And that means when you are being interviewed by them officially," he paused and then looked over his glasses, "And then when unofficially they come to your cell without me being here and offer you a deal and also threaten you......Do you understand me?" Smith looked deadly earnest.

McDonagh nodded grimly.

Paddy Smith then went through how he felt the interview and the next few days in the cell would unfold.

He had nearly finished when Sergeant Nixon arrived with Inspector Armstrong to begin the interview. It was to be done in the cell.

Three officers who were not local to Ennis accompanied Armstrong. Nixon looked uncomfortable, something that was noted by the small solicitor. Was this because it seemed his police station was now under different control? Either way, he would have to be careful in his approach to the police on McDonagh's behalf.

After the usual introductions, recording of time, place, date, and accused details being scribbled down, Armstrong moved straight to the heart of the questioning, hoping to catch his suspect cold.

"Why did you kill Seamus McDonagh?"

"I didn't kill him."

"But you saw him lying dead, there were no others around, who else could have killed him at that time of the morning?"

"I didn't kill him," McDonagh repeated.

"Why did you leave him?" Armstrong retorted.

Michael McDonagh took a breath, he had been told to admit to walking past the body. Paddy Smith believed that the witness was in all likelihood an informer who would have been in the hills while McDonagh was doing the IRA drills. So rather than deny it; honesty and transparency would unsettle the questioner.

"I was late back, and I was rushing to be home before Tom or me' Ma' were up. I thought he was drunk; I didn't know he was dead. Had I known I would have stopped."

There was a slight pause from Armstrong and was that the merest hint of a smile on Nixon's face, wondered Smith?

"Would you now? You thought a man lying down with his eyes wide open, blood coming from his mouth was just drunk?"

"Yes."

"Are you a fool? Are you an eejit?"

Smith raised his hand; Armstrong had overstepped the mark. Maybe this cold, northern detective was not quite as good as he thought he was.

"Could you ask Michael questions and keep your opinions to the tearoom, thank you."

Armstrong's face reddened as he looked at Smith. Smith glanced at Nixon, yep that was a smile on his face. The two officers of the law were on different pages.

"What were your dealings with Seamus Carville before his murder?"

"Nothing much, he was much older than me. I would talk to him in the pub and say hello. But he rarely worked in the field and well....his stories of his old life were a bit boring."

"Did your IRA commander not know of him."

"I am not in the IRA; I go to the drills because I enjoy them."

"But your commander, Sean Flynn seems to think you are in the IRA, why else would he be training you?"

Smith interrupted the interrogation, "You are leading him, Inspector Armstrong." Before turning to McDonagh, "Do not answer that statement, he has not established its relevancy to you committing a murder."

"Mr. Smith, your client as a member of the IRA will be ordered to carry out what they regard as military action. Therefore, it is highly pertinent as a motive for this murder."

"Mr. Armstrong, there is a ceasefire, a treaty is about to be signed in London. Everyone has been told to desist from violence. The IRA is no longer operational, and you know as perfectly well as I do that a few silly boys running up and down a hill, playing at soldiers does not an assassin make, Particularly if the assassination was via a complex poison rather than a bullet. Or are you now saying their early morning training involves a class in chemistry?"

Nixon's smile was becoming impossible to hide.

"Mr. McDonagh, you are in serious trouble, I cannot advise you to ditch your lawyer, however, he is giving you bad advice. We can help you. But you need to listen to reason. So for the moment, I will terminate the interview and let you consider your options." Armstrong looked sternly at McDonagh and angrily at Smith before standing up and leaving the room with *his* three officers.

Nixon slowly rose from his seat, sucking in his lips,

"That went well, Paddy."

"It did indeed, Eric, it did indeed."

"You know he won't stop, and you know what will come next."

"Aye, I do. I've told this young fellah what to expect, but I also know he is not alone when I leave here." Smith sucked his lips in the same manner that Nixon had a few moments previously.

Nixon nodded.

"I have asked for more information on the poison, strangely it's been slow to come across from Dublin. Not that I'm sure there is anything untoward in that." Nixon lowered his gaze from Smith.

"I'll leave you with your client, Paddy."

Smith was alone with Michael.

"You know what comes next, Michael, be strong. But that was a good interview."

15

The question that puzzled Robert Kelly was who the new witness could actually be. The police were unlikely to use 'oul' Dympna' again as her testimony would be untenable, yet this new witness had said nothing before. It was more than suspicious, he had colleagues previously in Philadelphia who had found new 'witnesses' late into an investigation. Kelly suspected the same was happening here. It was a kind of corruption. A minor abuse of the law that normally led to a good outcome....a bad person would go to jail. Which was all fine and good until it involved you. Then it was not so good. And this arrest of Michael fell into that category. Kelly was seeing the negatives more clearly now.

The number of people who were either in or arriving at the McDonaghs to offer support made it an uncomfortable place to be, not least for any Hotel guest to offer support.

For this reason, Robert Kelly decided he needed to gird his loins and for the common good return up the hill and talk again with the '*keeper of the well.*'

Maybe after go and see his horse.

Jack decided he had enjoyed his father's first conversation with 'oul Dympna' so much he would not want to miss round two. They wandered up the hill and discovered a small queue of tourists, who had bathed in the stream and were awaiting a drink from the magic well. Dympna was doing a roaring trade. Whatever conversation Robert thought he was going to have would be subject to a waiting time.

"You know what son? Why don't we have another swim in the stream, it'll be good for our skin."

"Dad your skin is sixty, mine is not thirty. I froze when we went in there last week, so no, I will sit that one out, but you can absolutely go and discover your youth again. I'm sure 'Whiskey in the Jar' will appreciate it later."

"Ah yes, that's a point, let's go to McFarlane's farm first, I'm sure 'Whisky' needs the smell of me and a gentle ride."

They walked the fifteen minutes to the stables where Bob McFarlane was mucking out with his sons. They were barely in their teens.

"Och Robert, if it isn't yourself," beamed Farmer McFarlane, "Wid'cha' be wanting to say hello to *Whiskey*?"

"I would at that, Sean," Robert responded.

Jack had to check his hearing, did his dad just say '*at that*' in finishing his sentence, was he turning into a local or something?

"Why don't cha' take her for a ride, she is in the last stable."

Robert followed by Jack walked to the final stable and there he stood, a brown chestnut stallion with a deep black mane.

"Is he not a bit big for you Dad?"

"You are not funny, son. Not funny at all," he opened the paddock door and led the horse out to the yard. He picked up a saddle that was in a group of five and strapped it onto 'Whiskey,' would you like a ride son?"

"No," Jack muttered. One accident in Ireland was enough, he did not fancy another one. His dad *unsupportively* laughed out loud.

"That's it son, just look at how your old man does it. And learn." Daddy Kelly was on a roll here. Then turned Whiskey away for a gallop and the horse duly responded by speeding up the hill, maybe a little quicker than Robert had expected. He turned the corner and was gone from Jack's sight.

Now what?

Jack returned to the stable and thought he should perhaps offer to help with the mucking out, but really he did not fancy it, so was hoping instead for a conversation on the arrest earlier of Michael McDonagh and the race the following day.

However, a Vauxhall 30 Tourer rolled in with a man driving at the front and a load of merchandise in the back seat. It was Brendan McManus.

He stopped the car in the middle of the yard and beamed with a huge smile, extricated his frame from behind the steering wheel. As he did so, some of the merchandise at the back, ended up in the front.

"Well hello Bob are you ready for tomorrow's race?"

McFarlane eyed him suspiciously.

"I am, at that Brendan."

"Have you many horses running?"

"There'll be the three of them, 'Whiskey in the Jar, Colonial Boy, and Inishfree.' Are you wanting to ride as a late entry?" McFarlane asked knowing there could be nothing further from McManus's mind.

"Ha, Ha, good one, Bob. Good one. With preparing three horses for the race, you'll be using up all your provisions what with keeping those horses groomed after a muddy ride, keeping your stables clean, and so forth. Well, I have some great disinfectant here, which can also be used to shine the horse's coat. And I could do you a deal, a special deal on repairing any injuries or cuts the horses may pick up with this super healing fluid........"

Brendan was an overwhelming force of nature, while he was spouting out his sales pitch, he was grabbing items from the back of the car and laying them out on a makeshift table he had put up in a flash. He knew how to grab the customer's attention.

And in this case, he did. Bob McFarlane's hesitancy was disappearing.

"Well, we have gone through a lot of stuff, I could do with not rushing to Ennis. Let me see what you have again."

Jack looked on semi-bemused at what he was seeing. Snake-oiled salesmen were as common as day in the US, but somehow here, it felt out of place. Things were done at a slower pace. Trust was earned and reciprocated. Brendan McManus did not fit this mould. He had a living to earn, and his mouth would be driving it.

"This particular detergent is great for getting rid of the smell, I can sell you five bottles for the price of four. Maybe I can throw in this handbrush as well. What do you think Bob?"

Bob put his hand to his chin, "I do need to restock" he mumbled to himself. This was taken by McManus to be a purchase request; he produced another bag and began to put the detergent bottles into it.

"Which handbrush did you say you wanted with the order?"

"I didn't say I wanted the order, Brendan." McFarlane looked at McManus with a 'you are pushing too hard look.' But this was one Brendan had seen over and over and over again. All he had to do was sweeten the deal, and then they would crumble, as they always did.

"So Bob I know how much work you have done for the race tomorrow. And maybe people don't say thank you often enough, but what I am going to do Bob, what I'm going to do Bob as a way of saying thanks from everybody in Lisdoonvarna and further afield, I am going to throw in a bottle of this special cut and graze liniment solution designed especially for horses." He handed McFarlane the bottle.

Jack recognised it immediately. Mary had been pouring it onto the gauze that was then put onto his head."

"Could I take a look at that, Bob, if you don't mind?" Jack asked.

The description was simple, 'Cure All Liniment' but the smaller writing indicated it was suitable for any cut without saying whether it was animal or human.

Jack looked from the bottle to Brendan and then back to the bottle.

"Brendan, my head nearly went septic because of this stuff. It may work for horses, but it sure doesn't work for humans. What is in it?"

"And that's why....Mr. Kelly isn't it? Yes, Mr. Kelly and that's why I am selling it to Bob here, sorry I mean giving it to Bob....for his horses."

"But you sold it to the O'Herlihys, they don't have a horse."

"I don't remember that."

"And now I am wondering who else you have sold this to as a liniment for people. I have a degree in Chemistry, I may be able to help you,"

"There is nothing wrong with this fine product, Mary and Jonjo may have misunderstood what it was meant for. I will visit them later and make sure they understand. Thanks, Mr.

Kelly for bringing this to my attention." McManus then returned his gaze to McFarlane; the closing of this particular deal had just become more complicated.

"Look Bob what I will do and I am only doing this for you, please, please do not be tellin' the others, but I will give you six bottles of the detergent for the price of four. And you can keep the liniment. What a bargain."

Bob again touched his chin, deep in thought.

"Well okay, let's do that. It'll save me a trip to Ennis. Boys grab Brendan's bag." He looked at his young sons and after wiping his hand on an already dirty cloth, put it into his back pocket and took out a one pound note with some coins, mainly sixpences.

"How much did you say that was?"

"Just the £1."

"H'mmm, I'm not sure who is doing a deal here," a suddenly hesitant McFarlane remarked.

"Bob, I can assure you when I arrive here again, you'll be wanting to double your order so pleased will you be with it. I can guarantee it."

The money was exchanged.

"Now what I will do is go to O'Herlihys and clear up that misunderstanding, Mr. Kelly here, has kindly advised me off. And if you weren't working Bob, I would gladly buy you a drink."

He took down his table as quickly as he had put it up and threw it into the back of the car. After jumping in the car, he as an afterthought requested that Jack give the starting handle a turn, it was that type of car. Several turns later a very tired right arm of Jack managed to enable the Vauxhall to jolt into action.

Brendan McManus was on his way back down to Lisdoonvarna.

Jack was requesting a pencil and paper as he wanted to make notes on the liniment, Bob told him to just take the bottle.

16

"Do you never leave this place?" Armstrong inquired of Nixon; it was approaching 8 pm.

"I could say the same to you. And your boys." Nixon looked at the three uniformed Dublin officers who were sitting at a different desk.

"I would like to talk with young McDonagh again."

"I doubt you will be able to persuade Paddy Smith to come out and sit in with you at this time of night."

"I wasn't planning to."

Nixon nodded, he understood and knew this was coming.

"Armstrong," Nixon began, "You will return to Dublin or Belfast or wherever you are truly based after this is over and continue with your life. I live here, these are my people. Protestant and Catholic. There is a kind of peace, incidents like this can ruin it."

"A man is lying dead, Nixon. My concern is to find the killer. And I think he is next door. And if he is not, I think he knows who the killer is."

Armstrong stood up and signalled for the officers to follow him through to the cells.

"Go home Nixon, go home."

Nixon thought for a moment, looking down at his desk papers,

"I have administration to complete, I will stay at *my* station if it's all the same to you." He could not stop what was about to happen, but by God, he could mitigate it. He had a science report to read.

McDonagh was lying on his cell mattress when the four men entered the room. One brought a chair and Armstrong sat down on it.

"You know Michael, we can do this, an easy way or we can do it the hard way. I think you want to go home to your mother and your brothers. You seem to have a tight-knit family. Don't you?"

"Yes," came the muttered response.

"That's lovely, but we have a problem here, don't we? A man has been killed, a man who did his level best to make this country safe from evil people. Yet it seems these evil people you've either joined or you are seeking to join. Which of the two is it?"

"I am not in the IRA, I just go to the drills,"

"But your drills involve charging up hills, using bayonets, target practice. Hardly a picnic with a couple of drinks, now is it?"

Michael remained quiet. 'Say nothing,' was the key message from Paddy Smith. He knew they would do this.

"So here's the thing Michael, if what you say is true and you did not know he was dead, and you just ignored him, it means we still have a killer out there, don't we? And that killer is likely to be someone who gets up early in the morning or stays out late at night on training manoeuvres, on drills? Because it's not likely to be any of the regulars at O'Herlihys, now is it?"

"I wouldn't know."

Armstrong smiled and murmured back 'I wouldn't know,' he signalled to one of the officers and nodded in McDonagh's direction. The soft approach had run its course. It was time to take a more direct route to obtain what he needed. It was regrettable that he had to descend to such exigencies but there was no denying how quickly results could be achieved. Of course, it was entirely justified. This was a murder case after all.

The officer threw McDonagh off his bed and proceeded to stand on his wrist. The prisoner screamed in pain.

"I'm genuinely sorry if that hurt, Michael, but you have to understand the nature of this situation. We have a witness who saw you by the body of a person the IRA would kill if they knew who he was. You are close to the IRA, so it really doesn't look too good for you. Does it?" Armstrong paused and refolded his legs. "Now we can help you walk away from all this, we can help you go back to your family, but you need to help me. You could tell me that yes indeed, you did murder Seamus Carville, or you could tell me which member of the IRA on the hills did it – and I will settle for you naming every name, we can investigate further from there or.....or I am going to give you another option Michael. You could work secretly for us, we would pay you an amount, which would make your life easier. Your mother would not need to take boarders in then, would she? All you have to do is continue with your normal life and keep us updated on who is going on the drills. We know Sean Flynn is the commander, but who is the quartermaster for your section, who are the corporals? How often do out-of-towners arrive to take the drills? You just say 'yes' and this nightmare comes to an end. So, what do you say?" asked Armstrong in a voice that he hoped mixed concern with steel.

This was the big question, Smith said was coming. He also said they would hurt him. Not badly but enough. They may leave the cell door open, but he was not to leave. He had to play for time.

"I'm not sure, I don't know. I did not kill Carville. I don't know. I need to think about it."

His answer was one Armstrong half expected, he nodded to the officer whose foot was resting on McDonagh's wrist. He pressed against it, McDonagh let out a yelp. He was then forced to stand and the three policemen, took it in turns to deliver punches to his stomach. He groaned with each one.

"Have you had enough time to think about it yet?" An unmoved Armstrong speaking in a low, even voice inquired.

"I don't know, I don't know. Let me think, please let me think about it."

Armstrong nodded again to the policemen, and they repeated the punches to McDonagh's abdomen. They were about to repeat the pummelling when a voice cut through the dim light of the cells.

"Detective Armstrong, it is 9 pm, I am locking the station up for the night. May I ask you and your officers to complete your business please?"

Michael McDonagh may not have known it as he lay on the floor bent double, writhing in pain but his beating had just come to an end.

Armstrong bent down and whispered in the prisoner's ear, "Yes, McDonagh you think about it, but don't take too long or I will ensure you swing on a hangman's noose."

The detective and his accompanying officers left the cells and returned to the office where Nixon was sitting. He did not look up when they re-entered, keeping his eyes firmly on the paperwork.

"Get what you wanted?" It was as if he was speaking into the desk.

"Not quite yet, but I am sure we will within a few days."

"If I could ask you to pick up your things and retire for the evening. Constable O'Shea will be on a late shift and will re-open the station at 8 am tomorrow morning. He is under orders not to allow anyone in before then and that includes visiting officers. Those are the constabulary rules, and we will not be breaking them." He paused before following with a query, "What time can we expect you tomorrow, and do bear in mind it is a Saturday?" Nixon inquired.

"Not sure, we have a couple of other leads we wish to pursue, so it may be closer to midday. Perhaps you could arrange for another formal interview with McDonagh later in the afternoon, say 4 pm. Maybe advise his solicitor, that Smith chap."

"I suspect Paddy Smith will be at the horse race, he may struggle to make that appointment time."

"Well no matter, you can sit in if you like, it will be a short conversation. McDonagh will be thinking over several new pieces of information that we have provided him with. He will be considering if we need to increase the flow of this information over the next few evenings to help him with his decision-making."

"Michael McDonagh has been accused, Armstrong. He has not been found guilty; he is a wee boy. I would ask you not to abuse the situation."

Armstrong smiled, "Sure,"

"You should also be aware that Paddy Smith has made out an injunction requesting the Resident Magistrate here, suspend further questioning until it has been established who the witness was, and a detailed breakdown of the science report is provided."

This stopped Armstrong in his tracks.

"Why did you not tell me that earlier?"

"I have only found it now, going through all my papers." Nixon looked down again at his desk.

Armstrong shrugged, "It will take a couple of days, the witness is subject to national security protection."

"You mean he is an informer?"

Armstrong's smile almost made Nixon shiver. It combined malevolence with a genuine desire for understanding. He said, "Goodnight Nixon, this is above the level of a countryside Sergeant, I'm sure you understand." He smirked as he put on his coat and walked through the door his officers had opened for him.

He needed a drink. But it would not be alcohol. He was teetotal as were his men. His culture was different from those he was now investigating.

17

The race was due to start at 11 am, it would run from the Spectacle bridge south of the town, then through Main Street, and loop around at the Ballyinsheen Beg, before finishing just outside the Corpus Christi Church. A race of four miles, which would last less than ten minutes.

Robert Kelly had enjoyed his ride the day before, 'Whiskey in the Jar' was a beauty to ride and very quick. He had walked back from McFarlane's farm with a bounce in his step. He would show his son that his old man could still be competitive. Oh boy! What an adventure! This was exactly why they both needed this trip.

Their walk back took them via 'oul Dympna and as it was becoming late, the queue of customers had disappeared. Robert had wanted an extended conversation with her, but he was tired, and they knew the McDonagh household would be fraught because of Michael's arrest, so a delayed return made sense.

'Oul Dympna seemed jollier than her previous self, she greeted the Americans with a big toothless smile. Today had been a good day.

"So yez want the waters for tomorrow," it was a statement rather than a question.

"Aye, that we do." Robert Kelly heard himself say, it was as if he had been infected with the language.

"Would you be wanting a blessing for your horse?" Inquired the old woman. This took Kelly by surprise; how would she have known he was riding in the race? He felt compelled to ask.

"You seem to know many things, Dympna...."

"It's in the waters and in my ears," she handed them two beakers and dipped the ladle into the bucket before pouring it into their cups.

"Are you aware young Michael McDonagh was arrested?"

"Aye, I was. It'll be for the best."

"Why do you say that?" A bemused Robert asked. Dympna smiled at the question, 'mere children.'

"The spirits are helping him, they're helping Maire." She paused and put the pipe to her mouth before taking a puff.

"You'll not understand." She murmured, but loud enough for the Kellys to hear.

Robert could not work out if he was angry or curious but saw an opening to probe.

"Not understand? I'm not sure there is much to understand. A man has died, two brothers have been arrested, one I think on the basis that you may have seen him. Seems pretty clear to me."

'Oul Dympna put her pipe down and looked the American in the eye, before looking away to the hillside as if caught in a dream.

"I saw a McDonagh, and I saw a bad spirit escape, it infects others, it infects the air. But I have made it right, as you will see." She returned her gaze to Robert, "Now, do you want my blessing for the race tomorrow? It'll be sixpence and another sixpence for the water."

Jack burst out laughing and was met with a scowl.

"D'ya want me to curse you?"

He stopped laughing instantly. You just could not be sure.

Robert dug into his pocket and fished out a couple of sixpence pieces. She smiled upon seeing them, it had been a good day.

"Take this pot and pour it on your head tomorrow morning and then on the mane of your horse. Say '*Spiorad Cuchalain*' when it goes on your head and then whisper into the horse's ear, and you'll be fine. The spirit will look after you both.'

"Er, yeah. If you say so."

Jack noted a bottle in her bag and found his hand moving toward it,

"*Whit'ya doin?*" Dympna demanded to know with more than a hint of anger.

"Oh sorry, I am just checking, we've come from McFarlane's, and he has just bought several of these bottles. He bought it for his stables."

Dympna looked at him with irritation.

"And I bought them to clean me' cups. People don't want to be drinking the sacred waters from dirty cups. What's wrong *wid'cha*?" She snatched Brendan McManus's detergent from Jack's hand and shoved it back into the bag, shaking her head as she did it. The cheek of these young people.

Robert decided it was time to depart but thought it useful to scold his son.

"Don't do that again son," he then smiled at Dympna, with a 'Young people, what do they know' expression, which was *half* returned.

They made their way back to the boarding house/hotel. It was now past six in the evening.

Maire was sitting in her kitchen with Tom. The other guests were in the dining room 'enjoying' a more potato-orientated meal than normal. It was an Irish stew without much meat or carrots or even *scallions* for that matter. Although the Kellys were never quite sure what scallions were, Maire had assured them it was an important ingredient.

The Hotel guests were aware of the arrest and therefore understood why the fayre was poorer than normal. But this was the West of Ireland, they were there for the weekend's events, which included the horse race and a dinner dance at the Hader Hotel, so were prepared to accept a couple of bumps on that journey.

Tom greeted the Kellys as they entered and invited them to sit in the kitchen away from the eight-person dining room. Table which sat proudly in the front room looking out onto the street. The Kellys were hesitant, not wishing to intrude on the family's difficulty, but equally wanting to avoid having to deal with Maire. They were however curious on whether there had been further developments.

"Paddy Smith has raised an injunction to have the arrest dropped on the grounds that the police have no evidence," Tom remarked.

"They'll have something, Tom, what is Paddy looking for?" Robert cautioned.

"Och, he thinks as there are little details on the cause of death and the motive pre-supposes so much what with the arrival of a new witness, all too much guessin' from the police, in his opinion, so he is going to force them to give him something, or have Michael released."

Robert nodded. The evidence seemed scant, but he also knew from his own experience that he would not give the defending attorney too much information, too quickly. If he had his man, he would look for time to build the case and not have it taken from under his feet with too early a technicality.

"Is Paddy Smith coming here any time soon," Robert inquired.

"He'll be here for the race, Tim will be the bookmaker and I think his dad likes to keep a wee eye on him in case he misbehaves." Tom allowed himself a grin.

"Would you mind if I talked to him about the case?"

"Talk to him, all you want. We'll take any help, we can get."

"There is a library in Ennis isn't there?" Jack asked out of left field.

Tom looked at him strangely, it seemed a bizarre question.

"Well yes.....but it is very small. You need to go to Galway City for a proper one. They have a University there, I think. Anyway, why do you ask?"

"I'm not sure, I want to check a few things."

Tom nodded and Jack noted that it was his dad who was now looking at him strangely.

Maire remained unusually silent. Her eyes were red, Michael had always worn his heart more on his sleeve than his brothers. He took an interest in politics without really understanding much of it. He was a boy in search of a cause and wrestled with the need to explore more than his siblings. Maire blamed herself. Mothers always do, it's another price of love. Things that are beyond your control and yet....yet somehow feel that they are within your hegemony.

The Kellys retired early for the evening as Saturday was going to be a big day.

18

Robert had been up early and managed to awaken Jack with his increasingly noisy stretching. He was taking the race very seriously. The grunting was shaking the walls. Jack rose from his bed to note that his fathers could barely go past his knees. The efforts continued to be made by Robert as he lay on his back, attempting to raise his legs straight into the air had changed from a grunt to a volcanic rumble.

God help the horse.

"Dad, I think we should go down for breakfast, I'm concerned you're gonna' break something besides my wish not to have to listen to you."

Jack quickly got changed and found himself still waiting for his father, who despite the early morning stretching exercises seemed to be moving more slowly. That had not done him much good Jack sniggered to himself. They both made their way downstairs taking it in turns to visit the outdoor toilet and then to the dining room for breakfast.

It was packed. Or at least had eight people all cramped around a large table. Word had spread that Robert was to be in the race, so he was clapped into the room. He smiled and dismissively waved his hand and squeezed in between his son and a forty-something spinster from England.

She thought she had struck gold.

The breakfast was as limited as the evening meal from the night before, where previously they had porridge, freshly made bread, bacon, and egg with something they called a 'soda farl.'

Today, they had the porridge but with yesterday's bread, yesterday's soda farl, and scrambled egg without the bacon. Maire was nowhere to be seen. Tom was running the show with Damian providing support. This was not their world. But the Hotel guests played along. Their expectations were set.

The conversation was convivial, nobody wanted to talk about the arrested family member of the IRA, who may have committed a murder. Yes, they talked about it in their rooms and wondered whether they should change Hotels, but what chance of that was there when it was the weekend? Everything was booked solid.

The focus was on Robert Kelly and the ride. He was fielding a lot of questions from around the table and whilst he just loved the attention, Jack was beginning to notice that his movement in the seat was rather stilted. A couple of 'Oofs' as he turned to speak to the spinster followed by an 'Aah' as he reached across the table for the salt indicated a man who had strained something.

All was not well in the Kingdom of Denmark.

When breakfast was completed, they all made their way back to their rooms or out to the toilet, for those who had delayed ablutions. Robert waited and put his hand on Jack's thigh to keep him sat down. They would leave together. After everyone else had departed.

"Jack, I have a problem."

"What have you done?"

"My back has gone. I am currently in absolute agony."

"Oh, God. You can't race then."

"I will have to, I cannot let Bob McFarlane down, he could have given 'Whiskey' to someone else."

"Dad, you've got an injury, bumping up and down a horse will make it worse. And that's assuming you still stay on. Which right now is a big assumption."

"I can't let the man down."

"Well, you're going to have to. I'll go now to the farm and explain the situation. He'll understand, he knows you're not so young....."

The 'not so young' phrase in hindsight was not the best phrase to use.

"What do you mean, 'not so young,' I've been riding horses for fifty years and can still do it, don't tell me I'm not young enough."

"I didn't mean it that way, Dad. You know what I meant." There was a certain steel in Jack's voice. His truculent father would have to accept he was not going to be participating in the race.

"I'll tell you what Dad, I'll ride 'Whiskey' for the family name."

"But you can't ride."

"Yes, I can....just not very well. Let's assume I won't win, but I will protect the family's honour. Actually, let's assume I will win because we have 'oul Dympna's magical water and that must mean something." He rolled his eyes at the thought and then noted his dad doing the same. They then both grinned at each other.

"Son, you've had a bad head injury, and you want to go up on a horse?"

"Dad, we were trained on horses before we left for France. Yes, I didn't particularly enjoy it, but I do know how to ride one. I will take it gently."

Old man Kelly was caught in a dilemma, he did not want his son to risk the ride, but he did not want to let Bob McFarlane down, what to do......what to do?

"Okay son, if you feel you can, then yes. But the second you feel unsure, it's unfair on the horse." He smiled at Jack, 'horse' was a codeword. Jack smiled back. He understood.

"Dad let's somehow get you upstairs. I think you are one who needs to lie on your back. I'll ask Tom if they have anything that might relieve the pain. Failing that, I'll go to 'oul Dympna, I'm sure some of her nuttiness could help."

"Not funny son, not funny at all."

Much to their surprise, Siobhán had a stock of aspirin at the shop, so Jack Kelly was able to go to McFarlane's farm, comforted in the knowledge that his father had some pain relief.

Bob McFarlane was disappointed that Robert was unable to ride the horse and was initially uncertain whether to trust his son.

"Your father had an instant relationship with 'Whiskey' these things take time...between a man and his horse, ya' know."

"Well, let me ride him around the yard and then you tell me, if 'Whiskey' will bond."

McFarlane saddled the chestnut, constantly patting the muzzle and whispering in his ear. Jack couldn't hear and what he did hear he didn't understand. It was in Gaelic.

"On ya' get," McFarlane handed the reins to Jack, and he quickly lifted himself by the saddle's bootstrap. He patted the mane of Whiskey,

"I hope you understand my English, boy." He gently remarked as he pulled the rein to the left and Whiskey started to walk. They circled the yard, a couple of times before McFarlane suggested that Jack walk the horse up the hill in a trot.

The trot seemed to be progressing satisfactorily until they reached the top of the hill and 'Whiskey' was able to see only flat green land ahead, for as far as his eyes could manage.

He was off. And Jack was holding on for dear life.

Ten minutes later, Whiskey decided he had enough of the morning run and returned to the farm. He wanted some water and a little hay. He had not had much of a breakfast either.

When they trotted down the hill, Jack could see the big smile on McFarlane's face. Both his sons appeared to be laughing. The closer he was to the yard, he realised, it was not simply an 'appearance of laughing' they were laughing....hard.

"Whiskey took you for a wee run, then. I think that means he likes *yea*."

Jack was not sure whether he was relieved, delighted, or as frightened as he had been ten minutes earlier when Whiskey had set off on the gallop.

"Yeah, that's good to know. I think." Jack grinned at the two boys, then to McFarlane.

"Boys, take young Kelly here into the kitchen and get your Ma' to make him a cup of tea, I'll prepare Whiskey for the race."

Jonjo O'Herlihy was out of bed early, it was a big day for him and the bar. It was rammed before the race – the benefits of having very different licensing laws from England, where this would not have been permitted – and it would be rammed after the race. The most profitable day of the year had begun. His beautiful daughter, Mary had been selected as the starter, she would wave a yellow ribbon to commence the race and would then hand that to the winner. With a large bottle of Brandy from the O'Herlihy vaults.

The pub also acted as the impromptu betting shop, where the bets would be placed. Tim Smith had set up earlier with one of his cronies a large blackboard with the horses and riders' names written on it and was placed in the corner of the bar.

There were five horses: Colonial Boy, The Burren, Mary's Child, Brian Boru, and finally Whiskey in the Jar. For some reason, Whiskey was trending as favourite. However, word was beginning to filter out that Robert Kelly was moving very poorly in the morning, would that impact the performance?

The betting was beginning to shift, Brian Boru had moved to favourite by 10 am. Whiskey had dropped to 3rd favourite.

At 10.30 am the horses assembled at the main square which acted as the parade ring, they would walk from there to Spectacle Bridge. There were gasps from those who did not know that Jack had replaced his father. Both the Kellys at this point were relatively well known in the town and as Robert had told anybody that would listen, when in O'Herlihys how he had grown up with horses, not a word had been mentioned about Jack. So no, this was looking less like a good bet. The gasps therefore included a few folk who were now regretting their wager.

They made their way out to the bridge with people lining the route. There were cheers, hat-waving, and a wonderful hubbub of noise. The horses were not remotely unsettled. A couple seemed to be enjoying the attention.

They reached the start line, Jack bowed to Mary, and she returned the compliment. Her luscious black hair was tied back with a yellow ribbon into a ponytail. She also wore a bright green dress. Jack thought it was something from a fairy tale, she looked that good, and in fairness to Mary, she knew it as well. It was not just her father's day....

Jack had poured the magical waters onto Whiskey's mane and whispered the magic words '*Spiorad Cuchalain*' into the horse's ear. It was now or never.

The timekeeper signalled to Mary and shouted to the contestants to ready themselves. They had been walking their horses in circles and now approached the front of the bridge. The tension was rising, then Mary threw her ribbon in the air and they were off.

The horses thundered over the bridge and the Aille River gorge below it with the early leader being Brian Boru. Whiskey was trailing in the rear. But Jack was frankly comfortable with that, he felt the horse was controlling him rather than vice versa.

The horses made their way through the town, Brian Boru was now being matched stride for stride by Colonial Boy. Whiskey was having its race with Mary's Child at the back. As they made their way out of town towards the Beg, the track became muddier and more difficult to navigate. This caused problems for both Mary's Child and The Burren, who began to fall back sharply. There was a sharp turn at the rock pile on the Beg and this caused Brian Boru, problems. He went far too wide and found himself, several yards behind Colonial

Boy. Whiskey was several yards again behind Boru in third place.

The crowd who had waved them off at the start had run as fast as they could back to the centre of town to see the race climax. It was packed, could this ten-minute race have gone any faster?

Whiskey was gaining on Brian Boru, but Colonial Boy seemed to be in a commanding lead, the finish line only a few hundred yards away. It was looking like a fight for second place, Jack urged Whiskey on but then felt his saddle loosen. The strap had become undone. Could he hold on?

The horse knew something was wrong, he began to slow down from a gallop to a trot. Jack pulled the saddle back to the middle and held the reins and the mane grimly. But no harm would befall him. Whiskey was in control. Although as Jack was to remark later, he wondered what the horse was thinking as The Burren and Mary's Child ran past them moving Whiskey into last place. Whereupon this point would be jumped upon by his father, who would happily remind the grandchildren that he had been the horseman in the family. Not their father, Jack.

Colonial Boy had won and as he had been the fourth favourite in the betting there were some big winners and they were letting the world know it, or at least their world, in O Herlihys. Tim Smith was grinning, he had managed the bookmaking to profit.

Mary was smiling with the crowd as Jack came in last. All could see the broken buckle of the saddle. The crowd cheered the young American and he raised his hand and then took off his cap, twirling it, before then throwing it in the direction of the Dolan sisters.

This caused a small unsisterly skirmish, but no (lasting) harm was done.

19

For something that had been the talk of the town with much preparation, the whole event had finished quickly. Starting at 10.30, it was now not even 11 am and those who were not returning to their homes were finding themselves going to the pubs or ad-hoc open-air drinking tables that had sprung up in Main Street for the occasion.

O'Helihys had a locals-only rule, but it was poorly enforced and as Jonjo was taking a cut from the betting book being run by Tim Smith, there was always going to be a large throughput in the bar. Bets had to be paid, but the winner was a winner for the bookie as well.

There was a full working complement behind the bar, Jonjo, Mary, Gerry, and Charlie. They were having to go at speed to keep up with the orders. After the initial tsunami, Jonjo took senior management action, grabbed a pint for himself, and made his way to the door. He would decide who came in, and let the young ones as they were fitter, work the bar. He needed to qualify the customers and those who were perhaps a little older and more likely to be one-pint sitters, would be excluded. He wanted spenders and more of the *'five pints of your finest, squire'* type customer. However, he broke that rule, virtually immediately.

Jack and Robert had approached at the same time as Paddy Smith was going in. Paddy would not have been there for the drink, but he had backed the winner, so his son owed him a few quid and he was making sure the son paid.

Important that the boy understood the facts of life, and they were that when it came to gambling..... it came way, way, way before family.

"You rode a fine race, young man," Smith complimented the younger Kelly.

"Thanks, I think the horse didn't need me, it knew what it was doing," Jack smiled

"And what happened to you, Robert?" He asked of the noticeably poorly moving former detective.

"Oh, I just reminded myself that I'm in danger of becoming an old fool," he smiled, grimly.

"It comes to us all, Robert, and well done for even thinking about it. I'm a little older and I would have had a heart attack at the thought." Smith smiled supportively.

"Now let me get you both a pint after I've picked up my winnings." He signalled to Mary, who using the dexterity of mind, sight, and hands, took the order, whilst dealing with another customer. By the time, Paddy Smith had returned, Mary had brought out three full pints. She was not accepting the money at this point.

"You're grand for now, pay me later. Too many to serve," She swept away after handing the pints over and giving Jack a quick well-done hug.

Smith toasted Jack and they were joined by Tim, who thought that was everybody paid who needed to be paid. The four of them talked briefly about the race before Robert's crabbiness caused by the discomfort came to the fore.

"You know, we went past 'oul Dympna yesterday and she gave us a blessing from one of her spirits, well that wasn't much use in the end, I'm in pain and you finished last, Jack."

he half laughed. His son shared in the laugh, Paddy merely smiled before saying.

"But what was the blessing, Robert? Was it to win the race? Or was it that the spirit was to do something else?"

"How do you mean?"

Paddy looked thoughtful, "Dympna's spirits don't do prescriptions, they move free. In other words, she would not bless you to win. Did you remember what she said?" Robert looked slightly dumbfounded,

"H'mmm, I can't remember exactly, something about the spirit looking after us......I can't remember."

"Did the spirit not look after you both, then?" Smith remarked after taking a slurp from his Guinness, that he had not intended to drink.

"How do you mean?"

"Well, Robert you're not the young man you were or indeed think you are. You could have gone out on the horse and damaged yourself much worse than you have, could you not? And you Jack, you fought to stay on the horse and the buckle came loose, the horse knew to slow down. I think 'oul Dympna would say the spirit did look after you both." Smith smiled at his own, to his mind, faultless analysis. The Kellys looked at him with a '*come on now*' doubtful expression.

"Ah, you people of the new world, where no miracles can ever take place, and yet, and yet there is so much in this world that none of us can explain. Allow me to think that maybe Dympna's spirits do have a place in God's creation." Smith benignly smiled at the cynical looks coming his direction.

He widened his smile in response and bowed his head slightly. Tim rolled his eyes, how his dad could embarrass him, he looked for support from Jack. Who laughed back at

Tim, the young American was enjoying the discomfort of another embarrassing dad, and son........

"May I ask what the situation is with Michael?" Robert switched the conversation, too many fairies in the one they were having.

"I will return on Monday, they have a case, but so do we. He's a silly boy who has made himself vulnerable."

"Is there a full toxicology report?" Jack inquired and caused both Paddy and Tim to look at him in a similar manner that they were looking at the older Smith a few moments earlier.

"A what?"

"A science report, a chemist's report....something that explained the cause of death."

"It was poison, not a lot to add. They have not given me anything that suggests how Michael could have got hold of the poison." Paddy Smith explained.

"Well, look, Mr. Smith, Paddy....I was told there was white fluid coming from Carville's mouth with the blood. This could be interpreted as whatever he took reacting badly to something already wrong within his body. And given the number of travelling *hooch* salesmen there are around here, something could have come from them."

"Maybe, maybe." Paddy Smith looked at the younger Kelly, "I will ask Nixon what he has, I'll even ask Armstrong and if they do not give it to me, I will talk again to the Resident Magistrate and demand, they make this evidence available. The RM will earn his money, this month." He smiled sternly.

Jack's thinking was now focused on a trip to Galway, and the University library. No point in raising hopes but he needed to get there first and was not sure whether to mention it to the Smiths now. They did do things differently here, after all.

It wasn't until 5 pm on the Saturday evening that Armstrong and his three constables returned to the Ennis police station. Two RIC officers were manning the desk, but they were under strict instructions to inform Sergeant Nixon if and when Inspector Armstrong arrived. They were also instructed to delay his access to the prisoner, Michael McDonagh. Or at the very least, try....

"I want to see the prisoner now and I do not need Sergeant Nixon's permission, do you hear me?" An irate Armstrong shouted at the two officers.

Constable O'Shea, the older of the two, he was nearly sixty, felt he had met Armstrong's type before, "We have our orders, and they will be followed, with respect.........sir."

Armstrong looked at one of his subordinates who was busy rustling papers in his bag, "Did you bring the authorisation papers?"

"I'm looking now, sir." The accent sounded more Scottish than Northern Irish.

"Got' em," He smiled like he had won a horse race.

"Right now, Constable O'Shea, you can take as long as you like to read them, but we are walking through to the cells and your young man here is going to open the door and we are going to go in, is that understood?" Armstrong was leaning over the counter a few inches from O'Shea's face. He was not going to be given the runaround by a Southern bog-trotter.

"You do not have permission to go in the cells, and his lawyer is not available." O'Shea offered in vain, but they were already through the door and pulling the young constable with them.

O'Shea sighed he had done what he could.

The cell door was opened, and Armstrong walked inside, he asked for the door out to the police station counter to be closed. This was now serious policing not dealing with the few drunk's variety that he felt O'Shea, and his ilk would be more used to.

McDonagh was sitting up in his bed, fear was etched on the young man's face.

"So you've had some time to consider your options. Have you come to the right conclusion?"

Paddy Smith's advice had been clear, '*play for time, keep playing for time. Commit to nothing, but if you have to give, do only the minimum and then imply you can be bought further with money.*' They would need to go back to Dublin for that authorisation.

"I need more time to think."

"Well, we're not giving more time." He looked at one of his assistants, "Ian put your supportive hands on young McDonagh's shoulders."

Ian did this and began to squeeze. McDonagh was in instant pain.

"The thing is," Armstrong began again, "I was there in Croke Park last year when the 'tans and the army opened up on the crowd. It was dreadful, it was murder. It's something I swore that I would do all in my power to make sure was never repeated again. When you see people killed, that stays with you. But here's the thing Michael, nobody would have been indiscriminately shot had the IRA not murdered fourteen of our people and then used the crowd at the match to hide within. They could have gone elsewhere, but they didn't. That was Collins and his IRA thugs, they killed those folk as sure as they were holding the guns. I don't want that to happen again, I can't imagine you want that to happen again, now do you?"

"No," McDonagh responded sheepishly, but beginning to see where this was going. Interestingly, Ian's grip had maintained itself at a certain level, whatever damage that could be done, had been done. It was no longer hurting. Armstrong resumed.

"That's good Michael, that's good. But yet you still do these drills and manoeuvres with the same people who caused this evil. You can see the problem, I'm sure. So I am asking for you to help us, to help stop this happening, to have the peace, this island deserves."

"I'm not a tout."

Armstrong raised his eyebrows and nodded to Ian, who then proceeded to throw McDonagh onto the floor and press the sole of his foot onto McDonagh's neck.

"You wouldn't be a tout; you would be an agent." He nodded again to Ian, who responded by kneeling and heaving Michael onto his front, before pulling the arm up his back, to the point of dislocating his shoulder.

"Michael, I need you to think about this harder and quicker."

The door to the outer office opened, and Nixon walked through, wearing his full RIC uniform with medals.

"This interrogation is to stop now. You are in breach of the law." As Nixon walked to the cell he saw the constable with McDonagh in an arm hold. "Release the hold immediately or I will have you arrested for assault." Then looking at

Armstrong, "Trust me, I will have him arrested. And I will prosecute."

Ian released his grip and stood back, looking at Armstrong for direction. Armstrong smirked at Ian and then looked at Nixon with barely contained contempt.

"What side are you on?"

"Justice."

Armstrong shook his head; a mixture of contempt and pity was written in his eyes. He could not understand why those from the same tribe did not want the same Ireland as he wanted. One that ruled itself, but was accountable to London, one that saw the importance of the work ethic, the removal of religious influence from the administration of the law.

Yet here he was dealing with someone who would respect the Lord's day in the manner he would; Church on a Sunday morning, no alcohol, sober reading of the bible. Why was he protecting this sympathiser of a paramilitary army determined by all means possible to stop what they both wished for? Peace.

He sighed.

"Our evening is concluded then." He looked at McDonagh, "We will not be going away, we have a case against you, and we will make it. And make it hard. Consider our conversation."

He then looked at Nixon, "I'm not sure you fully understand what you are doing, nor do I have the inclination to attempt to understand why, but know this, you are no defender of justice and after this is over, I will come after you."

"Then you better bring live ammo, your kind only seek division, I seek the law. Only the law. The King's law. Take your thugs and be on your way." Nixon was virtually snarling at Armstrong.

Armstrong nodded and signalled for his men to leave the cell, before looking first at Michael then Nixon,

"Michael consider what I have said, on Monday if I am lucky or Tuesday, you will be moved from here to Dublin. Sergeant Nixon will be of no help, no matter how he breaks the sabbath tomorrow by reviewing your case. I want you to think about that Michael." He then looked at Nixon, "And I want you to think about this as well Sergeant Nixon, trust me next time I am here you will not have enough *ammo*."

Armstrong partially bowed to Nixon and left the cell area. He walked through the station and ignored O'Shea as he left the building. His constables were standing outside waiting in the car.

"Gentlemen, we are not going back to our lodgings, we are driving to Dublin, I need a special warrant and Monday morning is when I will have it. Get me to Dublin before midnight."

20

The Kellys were not sure what to do. There was the formal black-tie dinner dance at the Hader Hotel for which they had tickets but leaving the McDonagh Hotel for the evening's festivities given Michael's incarceration, seemed inappropriate, to some extent even, a bit rude.

Tom insisted they went, but the Kellys suggested not, and then Maire *demanded* they went. She would not cook for them if they did not go. Her son being in a cell was her issue to deal with. Not theirs.

So reluctantly the Kellys dressed in their tuxedos, cardboard collars, bow ties, and white cotton bibs. They looked in the mirror as they adjusted their outfits. Jack knew he looked good, Robert on the other hand felt he looked at the peak of his powers, again. It was a sweet, sweet feeling until he moved his back, which was on the verge of seizing up. There would be no dancing for him this evening, he would have to settle for looking like a master of the universe.

And if not that, then looking a bit younger would do.

There had been some afternoon rain, it was the West of Ireland after all, and a carriage had been ordered to transport them the mile to the Hotel. With Robert Kelly feeling every bump every inch of the way. He was beyond relieved to step down from the carriage at the destination.

"Help me with these steps son, and I will need a whiskey as soon as we are sitting, a double. No water." He raised his eyebrows to Jack which indicated his current level of pain.

Jack judged this to be the 'high' stage with little left before it progressed to the 'very high' point of no return.

There were over one hundred people in attendance and the Kellys had been advised, that it would be a healthy mixture of single people and wealthier locals keen to enjoy a black-tie dress-up event. In reality, it seemed to be closer to ninety percent singletons, with only a few (older) couples.

Jack could see the Dolan sisters and Siobhán, but not Mary. His initial estimate suggested a 2:1 ratio of women to men. Normally he would have seen this as good news, but in Lisdoonvarna during the festival, this also meant more pressure. The girls would potentially compete hard with each other and if they 'won' they expected the chap to fulfil his end of the bargain by acting in a manner that the whole town would know, he would now be courting that girl.

Or *woman*, as once the courting began, they were no longer a simple girl, they had now qualified to stride into the world of womanhood.

So in short, Jack was planning on having a very hands-off approach to the evening. Too many complications.

Then Mary walked in on her father's arm.

For an instant, there was a hush. Jack could hear only two noises, his heart pumping and his dad's (un)helpful elbow into his ribs, as if he needed direction on where to look.

She wore a blue flapper cocktail dress, with white lace short gloves and a blue beaded headpiece. Finishing with Angelina-styled dancing shoes.

Every male in the hall looked at her in awe, every female with a combination of awe, jealousy, mild anger, and in some cases relief. The relief would come from the knowledge that this girl was out of the league of most men in the room, which was of comfort to those girls who had pre-targetted their potential beau.

Her eyes met Jack's, and he smiled and slightly bowed, by the time he had his head level with hers again, it was Tim's eyes that she was smiling at. Our Mary was a strategist, all plates would be kept spinning.

The seating arrangements for the dinner, saw the Kellys at the same table as Paddy Smith, his wife, and Tim, with Jonjo and Mary and for some reason, the matchmaker extraordinaire Willie O'Neil. Fifteen tables in total seated 6-8 people with some of the seats being little more than stools.

It was a two-course meal with the mains being chicken stuffed with the chef's special cheese creation and potatoes, and the dessert consisting of Hummingbird cake with custard.

Not very gourmet cooking, a point Robert shared with the table. The frosty look he received, indicated his opinion on the matter was neither asked for nor wanted. Jack allowed himself a little chuckle then thought it a good idea to add to his father's discomfort.

"When Dad talks about being in the Philadelphia police, he was really in the kitchen there, so he knows what great cooking looks like." Oh, how they all laughed at that.......as Robert politely smiled and began determining the best way to re-write his will.

The dining part was very pleasant, obviously, all cross-the-table conversation had to be shouted, such was the din in a room that was probably more suited to eighty, but everybody seemed to enjoy the various dialogues. There was discussion on the McDonagh case, with Mary expressing noticeable sympathy for Tom, particularly having to manage the hotel, his work as a foreman in the fields, and his 'er, difficult mother.

Tim regaled the table with a couple of stories on his carousing at Trinity College in Dublin, that Jack found highly amusing, as did Jonjo. But his parents less so, Mary politely laughed at the key moments.

Eventually, the meal was over, and the centre of the hall was cleared of its tables to make room for the dancing. A band had arrived midway through the meal to set up their instruments. It was a five-piece, running under the title of 'The Burren Boys.' The sight of the accordion was for Jack, not a good start. At any rate, Paddy Smith and his wife decided it was time for them to depart and Robert Kelly took up their kind offer to take him back to the McDonaghs. He had moved through the threshold to 'high pain.'

Jonjo however was going nowhere.

Absolutely nowhere.

He was dug in for the night and was on water. No enemy combatant would be getting near his daughter this evening. Which would make it tricky for Jack and Tim.

Mary excused herself from the table and joined her squad (the Dolans and Siobhán) for a cigarette outside.

The band struck up their repertoire and they were substantively better than Big P and *his Fiddlers*. Jack had decided they needed the re-christening after what Mary had told him.

The accordion acted as support to drums, clarinet, guitar, and bass with their music enabling the *Grizzly Bear*, *Turkey Trot,* and *One-Step* to start the proceedings. The first dance saw the girls in the hall sitting expectantly, hoping for one of the farmer's sons to approach them.

But no approach there came.

This event did not have the tight man-management control that the Priests and Nuns could provide at the parish hall. So it was an empty floor for the first dance, the second dance saw no improvement with the men focusing on ordering a pint and huddling with their male friends to discuss the girls, they 'could' rather than 'would' go after. They needed a couple of drinks first.

Confidence had to be found through the traditional route.

Willie O'Neil had seen this all before of course and knew how to dislodge the hesitant males. He took out his little notebook and started to whisper information into the ears of several girls.

Thus mid-way through the third dance, the seated girls were no longer going to wait and took each other up for a dance. They all had practiced with each other anyway, but this time there was a show they had to put on. Oh, how they laughed....and displayed what false joviality they could muster, all the while looking to the bar area, where a pack of men were hiding behind their beer glasses.

This was phase one of Willie's theory on matchmaking, put the ladies on parade and wait......So the One-Step made way for the Fox-Trot with many of the girls still unsure about this newly imported dance, despite intensive practice before the festival.

Eventually, the dam had to break and a few of the girls having had enough of being looked at took inspiration from Willie's advice and walked to the bar to grab the name that the matchmaker had suggested for a jig. Glasses were hastily put down, drinks spilt, the sound of '*cheeesus*' reverberated around the hall, and men were at last up and dancing.

Well, moving would probably be a more accurate description.

Tim Smith, Jonjo O'Herlihy, and Jack observed this all and found themselves in fits laughing at the sights they were seeing.

"You know boys," Jonjo opined, "I was a dancer in my day, all the girls chased me, you know." Jack looked at him, and then at Tim. They both laughed at the thought. But Jonjo was merely warming up, he had objectives with these two boys,

"So Tim, what are you planning to do with your life? Become a lawyer like your Da? Or a bookie maybe?" Paddy Smith's son hesitated, this was not the conversation he was expecting, so he thought he would keep it light for the minute, keep the old guy happy,

"Och, I don't know yet, I am back in Dublin in a couple of weeks, then I'll be in London. There are a couple of opportunities there that won't exist here that I want to look at. I'll see how they go,"

"But you are twenty-seven now, you must have a clue. No?" Jonjo pushed further.

"Well as I said, I'll have a pretty good idea by December, by Christmas. Ask me then."

"Is it that you want to leave here and live in a big city?"

"No, not necessarily. I'll play it by ear." Tim smiled at Jonjo, hoping the line of questioning would disappear.

And it did.

Jonjo shrugged and grumbled something about how he knew what he wanted at that age before he turned his attention to Jack. Somehow the young American felt the smile coming in his direction was warmer. Maybe he was misinterpreting it, or maybe he simply just wanted to believe it. He could not be sure.

"And you Jack, given what you've been through with the war *and all that*....Have you decided what you will make of yourself after you've finished this travelling *malarkey* with your Da?"

Tim smiled inwardly; it was his competitor's turn to face the interrogation.

"Nope, I'm like Tim. I don't know. But I suspect it will be in a laboratory."

"You don't want to be a cop like your old man?"

"Definitely not. Definitely. I had eighteen months of people shooting at me, that is enough for this lifetime."

"Could you see yourself ever living here?" Jonjo upped the ante.

"I had not given it much thought to be honest," Jack then turned the tables, "Should I?" Jonjo laughed; he had overplayed his hand.

"Well, it's where you see your life, son. It's where you see your life." Jonjo then altered the conversation slightly, "When did your family go to America?"

"You would need to talk with Dad, but I think it was my grandparents who left, my Mom however was from Wexford. We are going there after this. I'll know more. But at the minute Dad has some of the knowledge. You would be best to ask him." Jonjo nodded on hearing his answer. He was about to do a follow-up with Jack when his daughter, Mary, Siobhán, and the Dolan sisters returned, and they were ready to dance. Two of the sisters pulled Tim and Jack up for their first jig. None of this waiting for the boys to ask nonsense, these were sisters who knew what they wanted, and Sinead knew how to lead. The girls themselves could have been triplets. The red hair, which they always attempted to do slightly differently from each other, so that they could keep some individuality, but it never really worked. Deirdre, the oldest and by far the quietest with Sinead and Breda vying for being the loudest and most confident. The younger ones were slimmer than Deirdre and this may have affected the older one's natural shyness. She was the one who reigned over her sisters and acted as their guardian when they were out for the evening. Not that they went out very often, life was limited in Lisdoonvarna outside of festival time.

This acted as the final siren call for all the other young women to start circling their prey. One by one, pint glasses were put on the table and young men were peeled away to the dance floor. As Siobhán was pining for Damian, who was sitting at home with his mother and brother, and Mary had an interest in the two boys who were up dancing, they decided to sit just down with her Jonjo.

Willie O'Neil was beaming. It was going to be a busy month ahead.

The music began weaving its spell on Mary and she found herself grabbing Siobhán before jumping onto the dancefloor. Jonjo laughed, then simply smiled. He had quite the daughter.

The music set being played by the Burren Boys was broadly similar to Big P's. Just much better. The lead singer carried his notes in a different way i.e., tunefully. Definitely a step up.

The Dolans intermingled Tim and Jack for three dances before the boys' begging to sit down was acceded to. It was noticeable to all there that they were probably the only two males in the room who knew the steps. This would have caused some resentment among the other men, were it not for the fact many could not care. They were too busy trying not to look silly in front of their friends, whilst at the same time, keeping the interest of the girl. A lot to ask of a 30-something, fifteen-stone farmer's son who would still be living with their *mammy*.

The evening rolled on with Jack and Tim taking turns to dance with Mary and Siobhán. Jonjo decided as the clock struck ten, it was time for him to depart back to the bar. His daughter would be safe as indeed was everybody in the town. This was the West of Ireland; danger came in the form of uniforms of whatever colour. There were none at the hotel or walking the streets, this evening.

The band concluded their set at 10.30. There were strict rules on this type of thing, after all, 7 am Mass, required attendance, as did the 8 am, 9 am, 11 am, and finally midday – there was always a tea break at 10 for the priests. A hungover or dishevelled congregation was not acceptable and thus evenings had to be curtailed at the appropriate time.

The crowd dispersed into the evening, every girl who had 'got off their mark' with a chap, would be catching the disapproving eye of the priest the following day. Tim, Mary, Jack, and Siobhain walked, in that order, arm-in-arm along the street back towards first the pub, then the McDonagh Hotel. Paddy Smith had come with his wife in their pony and trap, so Tim had the car parked at O'Herlihy's.

Jack found himself mildly jealous as they left Mary and Tim off, Mary would go into the pub and Tim would drive off. Or would they? The thing was as Jack held Siobhán's arm for the remaining few hundred yards of the walk back to the Hotel, he could not look back to check. He could only listen.

And he did not hear the car starting....or leaving.

21

The Kellys had gone with the McDonaghs to the 11 am Mass. One of the younger priests was allowed to deliver it on what was the primetime slot. He had worked hard on his sermon, but both the Kellys were surprised that the Wedding Feast at Cana reading could have provoked such a fierce response against the 'demon drink.' He even squeezed in the seven deadly sins in his twenty-three-minute diatribe, the Kellys felt the linkage between vanity and pride was at best tenuous. But agreed that gluttony was particularly apt with lust and greed being useful additions.

Drink could always cause despair and anger in equal measure. So as part of their post-sermon match discussion, they were of the view the priest was on point. It was more the manner of how he expressed it, the vehemence, *nae*, anger in his voice as the phlegm from his mouth sprayed the front row like a Gatling gun.

They returned to the Guesthouse, where Maire had prepared a light lunch of bread, some butter, and cheese with a mashed potato concoction called 'champ.' Each of the residents took a scoop to their plate and ostensibly seemed to enjoy it. The Kellys, less so.

Arrangements had been made by the Kellys to see Paddy Smith in the afternoon. The McDonaghs were due to visit Michael in Ennis. So both parties had separate arrangements for what would be the same subject matter.

The Smiths lived in Ennistymon, a small town between Lisdoonvarna and the county town, Ennis. Their house was a large rambling cottage with a thatched roof and a stable that could accommodate two horses.

Mrs Smith had prepared an afternoon tea, which included jam and butter. All very civilised and twee. Interestingly Paddy's wife disappeared as soon as she served the tea. Her more traditional view was that as men would be talking, she had other things to be doing.

The talk initially was of the night before, with Tim giving nothing away on how it ended with Mary, 'they simply chatted a while,' before he returned home. Robert caught the eye of Paddy. Two older men who understood there was an unspoken competition going on with their sons.

"So Jack, I am interested in what folk have said to you on the state of Seamus's body, you think there is something odd about it."

"Look, he has died from some sort of poisoning, the post-mortem picked that up, I just don't understand how they think Jack McDonagh or even the IRA, would have the ability or access to the facilities to do it."

"Have you seen the pathology report?" Robert jumped in.

"The what?"

"The post-mortem report."

"Ah yes, that. We will have something shortly, I am told. I have asked for the case to be dismissed because of the slow response. I know Nixon wants to release it."

Robert Kelly nodded; he had done the same with defence lawyers in Philadelphia.

"But you know Robert, I am not expecting very much from it. They will grant me a 'right to know,' but it's very qualified. They're trying to protect someone here so they can exclude what they like and argue it's not relevant to the case. So Jack what you have understood to be coming from Carville's mouth and the implication of that is quite crucial." The older Smith advised.

"Well look, Tim and I talked last night, and we are going to go up to Galway tomorrow. Hopefully, we will be there by midday. The University librarian whom I talked to on Friday seemed to think they had what I was looking for; "A Manual of Organic Chemistry for Advanced Students" by Julius B. Cohen and "The Poisoning of Animals" by James M. Taylor. Given that there was no smell of garlic on Carville's body this is not arsenic poisoning. I think I know what it is but may be able to confirm afterwards. She also said she would ask one of the professors there if there was anyone around the department who could maybe help further.

Smith coyly smiled, "Go straight to the police station at Ennis, if you find this silver bullet." He then looked at his son.

"And don't hang around." He paused before re-iterating, "You heard me correctly son, don't hang around!"

22

Nixon knew it was going to be a difficult day. His values, his conscience, and his professionalism would be challenged.

The new Ireland that was forming was to his mind divisive, people were moving and in some cases forcibly to other areas of the country. He believed firmly in a united Ireland, but a united Ireland that was part of the British Empire. To his mind, this was the empire that represented the greatest contribution to the world since his Lord, Jesus Christ descended from heaven to announce God's reign on earth. As a good Protestant, he believed that hardship, work, and duty were the basis of life. Keeping the sabbath holy being critical. For this reason, he never truly understood why the Catholics around him went to their Mass and the pub or a Gaelic match on Sunday. That was neither holy nor respectful. For this reason, it was important that with the partition of Ireland, solid prudent Protestants such as himself had a *duty* to remain.

Yet, he found himself on that Sunday afternoon driving to the Resident Magistrate at Enniskillen House in Ennis town, thus breaching the fourth commandment on keeping holy the sabbath day.

The RM was on secondment, the previous one George McElroy had been murdered a few months earlier by the IRA pre-ceasefire. So the new temporary Magistrate, Douglas McDonald was wary of visitors and had a police guard permanently at the house. He slept with a gun under his pillow. The former RM, George McElroy had been a signed-up member of the Orange Order and hated Catholics as much as he hated Republicans, in many respects he saw them as the same thing making sure his judgments reflected that. Many younger people ended up in prison with little evidence.

Nixon did not like him, in his view '*silly wee boys*' playing at soldiers who then become dragged into a world they knew little of, a fight they do not understand, a destination they could not see should not be arrested and thrown into jails where they would learn from older, harder men.

It turned young men into hard men.

When Armstrong arrived with his Special Branch officers, Nixon could see history repeating itself.

McDonald had not been expecting him, Sunday was always very quiet but invited him into the drawing room of the large house, nonetheless.

"And to what do I owe this visit, Sergeant?"

"I need an injunction; I need something to stop Special Branch lifting a young man from Lisdoonvarna and bringing him to Dublin for interrogation. And I also need an affidavit that demands all evidential material be released to me on the murder of Seamus Carville."

McDonald sighed, he had a loose knowledge of the case, not least from being badgered by Paddy Smith on the matter.

"I have requested informally all the documents be presented to you and Paddy Smith and made the representations to the Lord Chief Justice of Ireland in Dublin himself, however, I've received nothing back."

"And you probably won't for another week. I fear Armstrong will be sat at the Chief Justices' underling's desk first thing tomorrow morning getting a warrant written up for

McDonagh to be taken to Dublin, which they will then serve on me tomorrow afternoon or Tuesday at the latest."

"You need something new then,"

"It's a trumped-up charged Douglas, poisoning is also not an IRA method of murder. If we had a proper judicial system this would have been kicked out a long time ago."

"That is as maybe, but right now, young McDonagh will remain under arrest here until they have their petition to bring him to Dublin. And then it will be out of my hands. For me to be able to overrule a petition from the Chief Justice department will require something new and without full disclosure, there is nothing I can do."

"The Armstrongs of this world will run away to the North when the partition is effected and leave us with even more division here. They are the IRA's greatest recruiters, they'll tell themselves they're not, but I've seen it too often."

McDonald nodded gravely.

"Will you stay on?"

"Yes, I want to. This is my home, it's all I have ever known. And my area has managed to avoid the worst of the troubles. There are reasons for that. Trust has been built over the years between Catholics and Protestants. But when outsiders come in and bring their half-baked politics....."

"I Know Eric, I know......."

Nixon nodded, there was little more that he could do, he would return to his home and attend the 'Evening Worship' service at his local church.

And pray.

23

The fifty-mile journey from Lisdoonvarna to Galway took Tim the speedster two hours to complete. There were moments when Jack thought his life was on the line. A combination of a racer behind the wheel and roads more suited to horses ensured Jack felt every minute of his journey.

They did however have a chance to talk, it began initially with their respective aspirations and Tim seemed to have a clearer idea of his before the subject moved on to Mary.

"She's a great girl, Mary, I am surprised she has not been taken yet," Jack genially remarked.

"Aye, that she is. I think she is waiting for the right chap. I'm not sure working in her dad's pub in Lisdoonvarna is necessarily the right place for her to find him."

"She never wanted to leave? She's not talked to you about Dublin? Or London?" Jack followed up,

"To be honest with you Jack, we've never had those conversations. I am in and out of life here in the town. My time is spent in Dublin, Limerick, Galway, and Cork. We always have a laugh in the pub, but we've never had that level of conversation."

Jack nodded. He found himself strangely pleased and yet felt slightly guilty.

"My Dad and Jonjo do talk though, and he thinks that Jonjo's loss of his sons makes it very difficult for her to leave. She is emotionally bonded with him. Remember also she lost her mother when she was twelve. All this must have an effect."

"Yeah, I guess it must." Jack thought immediately with his parallel loss of his own mother.

Then Tim cut to the chase and bluntly asked the question that hung in the air for both of them,

"It'll not be so easy to take her back with you to America unless her Da' agreed to go," Tim looked sideways as he drove at Jack.

The young American smiled, "And moving her from here to Limerick, to Dublin, to Cork is probably not the life she wants either."

They both found themselves laughing at this but laughing in a mutually supportive way. Mary was important to them, they both wanted what was best for her as much as themselves. Yet their lifestyles and locations made things challenging......and they knew it.

"I am probably the best option for her Jack. But until I decide if I really want to be a country lawyer dealing with a few cows being rustled and the odd punch-up in a pub, I won't be the best choice. And she knows that. Now that you have come along, that may change her thinkin' it may even change her Da's. Who knows...... when are you planning to leave anyway?" Tim added with a wry smile. Jack laughed heartily, he found himself being charmed by Tim's blunt assessment and honesty.

Evidently, they also shared more than their similar ages, they were both unsure of the point of anything. Marriage, permanent job, career, and children seemed like a foreign land and one they were not ready to visit.

Jack spoke to Tim of his time in the trenches, the fear and sadness of a war he could never quite see the point of. Tim spoke of seeing his friends split between those who fought in the same war with Britain and died on the green fields of France and the others who remained and then challenged

British rule in Ireland, many of whom also died as a consequence. Jonjo O'Herlihy's sons being the saddest example of this.

Both young men agreed, 'never again.' They were similar people but from different lands that now shared an interest in the same girl.

They arrived in Galway at 11:30 am and drove to the north of the city where the main library was located. Jack was surprised by how empty the place was, students were due to return the following week, which meant a librarian was able to help him find the books he wanted. Tim half-offered to help, chemistry was not his world however, but regardless Jack insisted he did and briefed him on the key things to look for, which was the impact of cleaning solvent in the body.

"I'm not entirely sure I've understood what you said there, Jack. Could you explain it in English this time," Tim grinned.

"Look for the word 'Arsenic' or 'Xylyl bromide' and anything that talks about cleaning detergent. Simple enough?"

"Aye, simple enough."

Four hours later Jack found what he had been looking for. A eureka moment. This presented him with the next problem. How could he take the book from the library?

The librarian who was very accommodating to that point, simply refused. He was not a student and that was the end of the matter. He could make notes, but no book would be leaving the Hardiman library. Both Jack and Tim begged her, 'There's a man's life on the line' line, fell on deaf ears. But such was the commotion that it attracted the belated attention of one of the senior lecturers, Thomas Dillon.

He had heard from the Professor of Chemistry at the university about a possible visit to the library on a matter of justice. This piqued his interest. After his morning's work, he made his way to the library.

"Youse' must be the boys Cecil was talking about," he boomed at the two younger men, even though he was not much older.

The librarian made the introductions as well as well as outlining the rules of the library about taking books out again to the two young men. Dillon smiled, Dervla was just the best librarian in the world for him. Nobody would be taking advantage of her.

He questioned the two younger men about the case and then advised them he had been interned in 1917 by the British, so was naturally inclined to support what they were doing.

Jack explained his theory to Dillon, whose smile seemed to widen.

"Would you like me to join you on your trip back to Lisdoonvarna? I think we have a miscarriage of justice being perpetrated here."

Tim and Jack looked at each other with big smiles and nodded their agreement.

"But you know they may not wish to listen to me, you have to be aware of that?"

"Why would they not?" Jack queried.

"Because the same people who are keeping this young man imprisoned on a trumped-up charge are likely to be the same people who sent me to a prison in Gloucester for a year."

"Ah, that could be a problem. But are they likely to know you? There were a lot imprisoned after the uprising." Tim responded.

"Oh, they will...and they'll know my wife. She was Joseph Plunket's sister."

Tim pursed his lips, yes, he could see how that could be a problem, Jack seemed slightly bemused these were places and names he was unfamiliar with, but looking at the two Irishmen, he understood all this may be a problem.

"Well given all that, are you sure it's such a good idea to come with us?"

"How do you mean?"

"Well, I don't want to be ruthless about this, but if you have been imprisoned once and you then act as an expert witness, will that not make you a bigger target?" As an afterthought, Jack then added, "And is your wife not likely to object to you placing yourself in that position in the first place?"

"Oh don't worry about her, as I said she is already a marked woman. Look, it's late now, you cannot be driving back this evening. It'll be too dark for that length of drive. Where are you staying?" Dillon inquired.

Tim looked at Jack, then to Dillon,

"Well, we were going to drive, it's not that far."

"Chaps, I will not be getting into any car this evening, I will go tomorrow morning. Or not at all." He paused. "Look, come back and stay the night, my wife Geraldine will make us tea and we can set off early."

It was Jack's turn to look at Tim then Dillon."

"*Aye*, okay then." Jack was mastering the local lingo.

Whilst the discussion on sleeping arrangements was ongoing, Armstrong was smiling to himself. They had arrived in Limerick and would stay there for the night.

Two cars had set out in the afternoon from Dublin with the expectation of arriving in Ennis by the morning. This would include an overnight stop at the city of the Shannon River. There were four Special Branch officers plus Armstrong. They were well-armed, each had a pistol and the latest *Remington* rifles, which had pump action capability. They stayed at the military barracks in Limerick for the night. It would be safer. Tomorrow was going to be a long day, with a seven-hour journey from Ennis to Dublin beckoning.

They had been at the Chief Justice's Office in Dublin at 9 am that morning and had their petition and warrant agreed by 11 am. Michael McDonagh would be returning with them to Dublin. For Armstrong, this would ensure he could be properly turned and become an asset to the state. It was a good start to the week when he could see justice being served.

Mary and Siobhán were sat in the empty pub talking, it was half an hour before opening time. Siobhán had walked with Damian to the field. Michael may be in a prison, but the McDonaghs still had to do their work. And Tom was going to make sure that Damian was focused on that rather than the understandable anger, the family was having to control.

Tom had the grace to allow Siobhán to walk with Damian without the need for an unwanted third string to the walking bow. Not least because he knew Willie O'Neil was now taking control of their courtship. He noted the grin on his younger brother's face when he was kissed as they reached the field by the girl he was now officially in love with.

Siobhán had skipped down the hill with a huge smile and bright 'hello' to everyone she met. Ah, to be in the first flushes of true romance. Recognised by others, respected even. She was now a woman.

In love.

And boy, was she flooding Mary with this 'love' as they sat holding their cups of tea. She would not be this way with Willie O'Neil, it would be a bit more guarded. But with Mary, there was so much to say, and Mary had to know every detail of it. Every. Single. Detail. Including the palpitations.

"It's too early to be talkin' about marriage, though Mary. Too early." Siobhán gushed.

"But your Ma' was married at 18, wasn't she?"

"Yes, but it was different then." Siobhán grinned as Mary laughed out loud.

"Anyway, what about you Mary? Those two boys are swooning after you and according to Damian, Tom is sweet on you as well."

Mary trying as best she could to control her modesty, allowed an embarrassed smile.

"Oh, I don't know if they are that interested in me,"

"They are Mary, they are." Siobhán gushed.

"Well Tim probably has a girl in every town in Ireland and Jack will be going back to America where he will have the whole of that country to choose from. And I really like Tom, I really do. But we've grown up together, I feel like he is my big brother and more so since....since," her eyes reddened, it did not take much for any memory of her own brothers to cast a pall on her thoughts.

Siobhán had seen this before and felt able to keep the conversation on track but move her away from the sadness.

"He is sweet on you Mary, and he would make a wonderful husband. You Da' likes him as well. He could run the pub."

"He doesn't really drink, Siobhán!" Mary laughed at her little joke on the irony. "He wouldn't know how to have four sets of pints on the go for three customers at the same time. He would tell them to wait their turn. Or he would kick them out." Mary was laughing as she imagined the scene. "He likes his way of doing things and you can't really have that in a pub when it's full. And anyway, I'm thinking Deirdre Dolan has a soft spot for him, I wouldn't want to antagonise her or any of the Dolans for that matter." Mary smirked.

"I'm serious," Siobhán persisted despite laughing, "We could have a double wedding, wouldn't that be great? Just great."

"I thought you said it was too early to be talking about marriage, make up your mind." Mary retorted, "I like Tom, maybe I might. But not yet."

"Would you ever consider leaving Lisdoonvarna Mary?" Siobhán queried.

"I don't think so, I don't know. If I wanted to marry someone really, really, really eligible, then I would have to. And I know I'm not getting any younger, but with Da' and the pub, it's not so easy. I'm not sure I even know what I want."

"An American." Siobhán laughed as she made the statement rather than the question then added after a suitable pause.

"Or a playboy."

She then covered her mouth as if she had uttered the worst of pejorative words that ever existed. But this sense of guilt seemed to then be overridden by the shrieks of laughing she and Mary found themselves engaged in.

Girls will be girls. From the city to the countryside, girls will be girls.

24

It was just after 11 am before Special Branch arrived at Ennis police station. The Dublin police car parked itself outside the main entrance. Two officers with rifles positioned themselves between the doorway and the car looking out to the main road, safety catches off. Just in case.

"Sergeant Nixon, what a surprise to see you here, and Mr. Smith. The great and good of the county." Armstrong smirked then changed it into a smile. "I have here a warrant for the removal of Michael McDonagh to Special Branch as part of the 'Restoration of Order in Ireland Act' so if you could kindly have the prisoner escorted from his cell and into the hands of my officers, I would be grateful."

"May I and Mr. McDonagh's lawyer see the papers." Nixon was determined to make this difficult. Armstrong handed him the papers, albeit begrudgingly.

Nixon read through the two-page petition, the warrant, and the supporting documentation quickly before handing it to Smith, who rapidly digested them.

"It says here 'that having furnished the local authorities with all relevant information, the accused is required to be transferred to Special Branch control.' You haven't furnished me with all the information. The doctor's report is incomplete. There is no information on the poison used, how it was administered, and how it caused the fatality."

"Mr. Smith, don't be funny. You have a medical report, that is all you need. That is all we are required to supply you"

"The medical report says Seamus Carville died from a poison that caused a seizure, represented by foaming of the mouth." It does not say, what the poison was or exclude the possibility of an underlying health condition."

Armstrong looked at Nixon and ignored Smith.

"Sergeant Nixon, could you please hand over the prisoner into our custody." It was said with a formality that belied the previous engagement.

Nixon did not move. He stood looking at Armstrong and slowly began to shake his head. Armstrong then looked at the two local policemen who were flanking the Ennis Sergeant.

"Boys, fetch the prisoner. Sergeant Nixon is in breach of his duty and if he persists, I will have to ask you to arrest him for preventing the lawful execution of a warrant."

"Don't move officers," Nixon responded.

Armstrong looked at his two Special Branch men and nodded in the direction of the door where the holding cells were. They opened the counter and walked through the entrance. One of the men took the cell key from the hanger just inside, where the four cells were located. Guns were shown.

The Special Branch man opened McDonagh's door and produced handcuffs which were swiftly applied.

"You're coming with us son, the bright lights of Dublin beckon."

McDonagh was pulled roughly out of the cell and into the reception of the police station.

"I'm not sure I understand why you are being so difficult Nixon, are we not on the same side?"

"I'm on the side of justice, you're not concerned about the innocence or guilt of this boy, I am. And what has been provided is weak. You have other motives, I know, But this is my area, I know these people, I know this boy. He is no murderer."

"Well, let us see, who knows it may not even come to trial," Armstrong then looked at McDonagh, "That will be up to you, son, now won't it?"

McDonagh remained silent, Smith was seething.

"You're a bad man, Armstrong, there is no evil you would not consider if helped you. Stay strong Michael, stay strong. We will get you out."

Armstrong had turned towards the door but stopped, he wanted to address Smith and his insult.

"I seek only to stop killing. You live in the world of unicorns. I have buried too many colleagues and I have witnessed too many funerals, aye, even of the other side. I will do what I have to do to stop it. The evidence says what it says. We will test the evidence by interrogating him in the real world, not in this *culchie* town." He made his way out to the car. The Leyland Charabanc was too big for the need to transport one prisoner, but it enabled more weapons to be stored in case of ambush. Every policeman was potentially a target and Armstrong knew he was higher up on any potential hit list.

They left for Dublin. It would be a seven-hour drive, there would be no overnight stops.

Paddy Smith's car with his racing son left Galway at 8 am. They arrived in Lisdoonvarna 11 am where they took the opportunity to re-fill for petrol and Jack to explain to his father what they had discovered. He also introduced the third person in the car.

Robert insisted on joining them for the final leg of the journey to Ennis. He had special knowledge and maybe, just maybe he did not want to miss out on something. He was not quite sure what his special knowledge could contribute, but that was incidental and secondary to this self-appointed *legend* of the Philadelphia Police Department.

The four of them were now on the road to Ennis. Small carts and traps with horses were passed with the horses being as startled as their owners. Robert threw up his hand to those they passed as he sat in the back seat as a form of apology. Tim was focused on his driving whilst Jack was praying like he had never done before on arriving at the police station in one piece. Dillon on the other hand was highly excited. His focus on developing the chemistry department at the University had taken him away from the excitement of the fight.

Within the hour they were pulling up outside the Ennis police station, Jack with no small amount of relief, jumped out of the car while it was still moving to open the door for Dillon. No seconds would be wasted in this pursuit of justice.

They ran up the steps with Robert Kelly following a short distance behind. The journey had not helped his back one bit, but he was not regretting this particular adventure.

They had arrived too late.

Michael McDonagh had been on the road to Limerick for half an hour.

"Look there is no way Michael McDonagh could have killed Seamus Carville. No way. It would have required him to force the fluid into the man and therefore there would have been marks all over his body of a struggle." Jack Kelly began.

"The poison used here is common in cleaning fluids, in detergents. Efforts are being made to have it banned because of deaths in England and I think the United States." The Galway Lecturer of Chemistry added, "And further, this could only have been taken orally. The ingestion time required for the poison to work suggests it would have taken thirty minutes to an hour for it to have caused a seizure if there was an underlying condition. So if he was up early for some reason and from somewhere he has taken the fluid. It will have been an accident." Dillon paused, before making a request, "May I see the autopsy report?"

Nixon was leaning on his desk with the younger versions of Kelly and Smith pressing on the other side and this man whom he had never met before, Thomas Dillon talking at him with an assuredness of judgment that could only come from his position. He went to the filing cabinet in the office and returned with the very thin autopsy report.

Dillon scanned through it and whilst he was doing this, Paddy Smith pondered on the next steps.

"This is new evidence that an expert witness in the form of Mr. Dillon can swear on, we may be able to get to Douglas McDonald the RM, and have a warrant signed for Michael's return here." He paused before adding, "We need it now as it may not be enough, once he is in Dublin."

"Can we stop them getting to Dublin?" Jack queried.

"I don't see how. And even if you did stop them enroute, they would just ignore the signed warrant." Nixon advised.

"What if McDonald was in the car with you Eric, and he is presenting it to Armstrong, he would not be able to refuse the release of the prisoner to our hands, surely?" Remarked Paddy Smith.

Nixon appeared to ponder the logistics.

"They'll not stop at Limerick, but I suppose they may stop for petrol at Nenagh, and they would be more likely to stop at the barracks there. I could ring Ken O'Reilly, the Sergeant there to delay them, they may of course choose to ignore."

"You better start making those calls," Smith determined.

Ten minutes later, the police car was leading the Sunbeam Tourer to the house of the Resident Magistrate.

"This is persuasive, Eric. But Mr. Dillon you do have the type of background that will make your evidence challengeable," McDonald made the remark that troubled Nixon the most.

"I am a Professor, my view can be challenged by other professors or indeed the Chief Justice in Dublin. But it would have to be on my facts, not my history. And I can't see who can challenge it. Even in this thinnest of thin autopsy report, the statement, that 'the complexity of the poison would indicate potential development for industrial use' should have frankly stopped even the arrest. But this allied with 'No distinguishing signs of a struggle with the deceased,' how the warrant was ever signed, I do not know. In the *new Ireland*, I would hope for a greater application of justice."

Nixon looked at Dillon with mild contempt.

"That's the type of nonsense Mr. Dillon that makes me see Armstrong's view. Your republicanism is as much a unicorn as he accuses me of believing in."

"Indeed," McDonald echoed Nixon's view. "Focus only on the facts, Mr. Dillon. Only on the facts."

Dillon with some assistance from Jack Kelly outlined the most likely cause of the death having read how the poison had reacted internally within the body of Carville. McDonald was satisfied without doubt of McDonagh's innocence but was reluctant to accede to the request of joining Nixon in the police car and journeying to Nenagh in the hope, rather than the expectation that Armstrong would have been held up there. Nixon however, had a persuasive argument to offer on that issue,

"Douglas when word gets out about what has happened here, no one will dare touch you. Michael Collins, and Eamon De Valera themselves will be carrying you through the crowd to acclaim. You'll be a legend, a hero in these parts.

"That is very true," Dillon added with a rueful smile.

Douglas McDonald raised his eyebrows, with a 'You're selling me a pup' expression, but then thought better of it. It would make him feel safer than the current and rather minimal round-the-clock protection he received from a solitary police officer. Who knows, maybe it would give him a place in local history if not national, as a man who stood for justice with neither fear nor favour. So maybe, just maybe, it was time for an adventure.

Summoning all the pomposity that any Dublin-appointed, Oxford-educated, Resident Magistrate could, Douglas McDonald looked at the expectant lawyer, professor, police sergeant, and two American tourists (what were they doing there anyway?) and muttered his decision,

"In the name of the King and the Justice I here serve, let's go to Nenagh and hope........" He paused, before adding with a half-smile, "And if we don't meet them there, we can go onto Dublin."

Paddy Smith looked at Eric Nixon. They both raised their eyes to the sky, no they wouldn't join him in the car for the journey. The thought of drowning in his pretentiousness was just too high a risk.

There were now three cars on the road to Limerick before the sharp left turn to Nenagh. Two had to stop for fuel and a check of the tyres. Paddy Smith's car had taken a beating over the last 24 hours and needed neither. Tim Smith knew and loved his cars. The mechanics of the Sunbeam Tourer he was driving were etched into his brain. If this adventure taught him anything, it was that he was not going to become a lawyer at this point. Racing driving would be his next port of call when the matter in hand had been dealt with.

It took two hours to Limerick and a further hour to Nenagh. It was 4 pm when they arrived at the police barracks. They were not prepared for what awaited them as they entered the courtyard of the rectangular base.

Armstrong's journey had been without incident. They had stopped briefly outside of Limerick for fuel and were proceeding at a satisfactory pace. The prisoner, Michael McDonagh was very quiet, they had tried to rile him, 'It'll all change for you when you're working for us.' Mixed with a few, 'You'll be a rich boy very soon,' at no point was the death of a man for which he had been accused, the topic of conversation.

As they approached the outskirts of the town they came upon a police checkpoint. There were three police vehicles and several policemen with, it was noted by the Special Branch Officers a couple of police rifles pointing at the small queue of cars from the hill to the side of the road. There had been ambushes before by IRA posing as policemen, so they were on their guard. Safety catches off, hands on weapons.

Armstrong remained calm at the front and within a few minutes they were being asked for their particulars, it seemed the Nenagh police were as concerned about an ambush by the IRA masquerading as Special Branch as they were with ordinary police.

"It is nice to see you chaps out patrolling the roads, they don't respect ceasefires those republicans."

The Nenagh police constable half-smiled and then looked at the number of non-uniformed officers who handed over their identifications.

"We are transporting a dangerous republican to Dublin for further interrogation, if you could hurry yourself along, we would be grateful." Armstrong half-smiled back in the type of condescending manner that any uniformed officer would detest when dealing with members of Special Branch or any 'Special' branch of law enforcement.

"Aye, well, we'll see about that." He abruptly turned round and walked twenty yards to a police car that seemed to have two men sitting at the front.

"What's he doing Mervyn? One of Armstrong's men shouted from the back of the charabanc. Armstrong looked round and shrugged his shoulders,

"I'm sure we'll be on our way shortly, they may have some intelligence on IRA movements."

Ten minutes came and ten minutes went. Armstrong had enough, he stepped down from his car and marched to the police car that had two men in the front with the officer who had taken their papers talking through the window.

"What is the meaning of this hold-up? We have urgent business in Dublin." Armstrong rasped, initially looking at the officer he had engaged with earlier but then looked across at the other two men sitting in the front seats. He specifically kept a gaze on the red-faced, grey-haired fifty-something man in the passenger seat. The sergeant stripes were visible.

O'Reilly looked back and then returned his eyes to the papers in front of him.

"Is this some kind of joke, Sergeant?" Armstrong was now speaking through the window at the non-responsive senior officer.

Eventually, O'Reilly decided he had better return the gaze, before sighing.

"Nobody informed us a suspected murderer was being transported through Nenagh. Nobody informed us that the Special Branch was doing this. It puts my men in danger when these things happen. And looking at these documents, I am not sure they are in order."

Armstrong's anger was moving in different directions. He was annoyed with the hold-up, he was annoyed with what he felt was a high-handed approach of the policeman who had taken the documentation initially from his car. Now he was moving beyond being livid by a country bumpkin pensioner sergeant who seemed to think he was God Almighty.

"You're not sure they are in order." Armstrong uttered in a barely credulous low voice and then he repeated the statement, "You're not sure they are in order?" raising his voice at the end to indicate a question. "May I ask your name Sergeant?"

"Certainly, it's Sergeant Ken O'Reilly. And I see you are Inspector Armstrong from Special Branch according to this document."

"Yes indeed, so you understand that I out-rank you."

"That, I do."

"So you will understand if I ask you to give me back my papers and allow us to proceed."

"Well, that's where we have a small problem, Inspector Armstrong. I am struggling to believe the dates on your documents."

"Sorry, what?"

"The dates on your documents. It says here they were signed yesterday late morning in Dublin, and I am being asked to believe that by 3 pm today, that is now, you've been all the way to Ennis, completed the administration there, and have now driven here in just over twenty-four hours."

Armstrong looked at O'Reilly, not sure if he was dealing with an idiot or something more sinister.

"O'Reilly, give me the papers back, we are going to be on our way."

The Nenagh sergeant was in no doubt that this indeed would be what Armstrong would do, but unfortunately for the Special Branch Inspector, one of his men came running from his car.

"Inspector, Inspector, one of our wheels has a flat."

Armstrong turned to the young Special Branch man with a look that indicated he felt that he was surrounded by imbeciles,

"Well, put the spare wheel on then for goodness sake."

"We can't sir, it's flat."

Armstrong's face was now the colour of O'Reillys, save for the fact that O'Reillys was permanently red. He returned to his discussion with the Nenagh Sergeant.

"O'Reilly, I need you to provide me with a tyre and I need you to provide me with it right now."

Was that a hint of a smirk on O'Reilly's face, thought Armstrong.

"Inspector, we will take you, your men, your car, and the prisoner back to the barracks in Nenagh, where we will review your papers by contacting Dublin and then replace the tyre. It will not be done at this checkpoint. However what I will do, on your behalf is, I will wind-up the checkpoint and we will all return to Nenagh."

O'Reilly finally removed himself from the car and ignoring Armstrong, ordered his policemen to close the checkpoint and return. He signalled for two of his team to come over for special instruction.

"Good work chaps, now take their charabanc back to the barracks. When you get there find or create another problem for them." His knowing wink indicated complete confidence in his team.

"Perhaps Inspector Armstrong, you would wish to travel with me back to the barracks."

"I'll go with my men," was the curt response.

"Well, it will take a while for the ropes to be attached to your charabanc, it would be more comfortable with me. You would be having a cup of tea in fifteen minutes."

"As I said, I will go with my men and the prisoner."

"Please yourself, see you within the hour."

O'Reilly returned to his passenger seat and adjusted his cushion. No point in travelling without some comfort.

25

Word was spreading in Lisdoonvarna that Michael McDonagh was being moved to Dublin, but equally quickly another story was developing that he was about to be released. O'Herlihys was buzzing with both stories. Somebody had talked to Tim Smith at the petrol station, and he said such and such, whilst another customer talked of seeing over thirty Special Branch men surrounding Ennis police station, taking Michael away and holding guns at Sergeant Nixon.

It came to the point that Jonjo considered opening a book before remembering the last time he did this without Tim Smiths' help, he had made a loss.

Mary excused herself and went up to the field where she knew Tom would be, she saw him bailing hay from the morning's scything session. He was a strong man.

She signalled to him, and he seemed to say something to one of the chaps, before wiping his brow and stepping down from a cart that he had secured the bale on. He moved across the field in a slow, graceful manner. Every inch a man.

"Hello Mary, is everything okay?"

"We've heard so many things about Michael, nobody knows what has happened, have you heard anything?"

"Well no, Paddy Smith was talking to the magistrate, he was not sounding too hopeful. And I know Jack Kelly and Tim were going to Galway. But no, I have heard nothing."

Mary was uncertain what to say, she wondered why she had gone up to the field anyway. It seemed to her now, it was as if she was looking for gossip. But in her heart, she knew it was not. Tom needed to know he was not alone; that people did care and were looking out for him and his family. More specifically, Mary cared and wanted him to know that. She decided against repeating the more extreme stories that had been heard in the pub and settled for reporting to him that Jack and Tim had returned and had then set off for Ennis. She believed they had reason to do so, there was a reason to pray....and hope.

Sergeant Nixon's police car was the first to enter the Nenagh barracks followed by the Ennis Resident Magistrate and then Tim Smith with Jack Kelly, Robert Kelly, and Thomas Dillon in it. There in the corner of the parade ground was the charabanc that Inspector Armstrong had been driving, hoisted up, minus a wheel and the front engine bonnet uncovered.

They could see Armstrong attempting to argue with O'Reilly who seemed to be spending his time merely shrugging his shoulders. The other Special Branch men were in different states of agitation with Michael McDonagh cuffed to one of them.

Eric Nixon waited for McDonald to dismount his vehicle before striding across the barracks yard to where Armstrong and O'Reilly were.

"Well, we do seem to have a fine situation here," beamed the Ennis Sergeant looking at Armstrong's car. The Special Branch Inspector grimaced; he had a feeling that his day was to become a little worse. Once more, he was failing to read fully the situation. His day was not just going to become a 'little' worse, it was about to dissolve.

Addressing his fellow police officer first, he said in a voice that he hoped did not betray the apprehension he felt.

"Sergeant O'Reilly, I have here Mr. Douglas McDonald the Resident Magistrate for the county of Clare, and he has signed this warrant for the return of Michael McDonagh to the Ennis police and further that he be released pending further investigation into the death of Seamus Carville."

"Well now, that seems to change the situation," O'Reilly remarked, mustering as much gravity as he could looking at Armstrong. The man was intimidating and no mistake, he thought, but he was going to go back empty-handed, or my name is not Kenneth Aloysius Eugene Loyola O'Reilly.

Armstrong could not hide the sneer in his voice when he said, "Oh, I don't think so, a warrant signed by the Dublin Chief Justice trumps anything that colluded efforts from culchies, and foreigners can come up with." The contempt he felt for these country folk poured from his eyes like molten lava. Who were these people to question him? It was laughable. He couldn't wait to leave them to the relentless brutality of their existence.

"And that my friend is where you are wrong," responded the Resident Magistrate. The Special Branch man's eyebrows nearly shot off his forehead. However, the Resident Magistrate was only getting warmed up. There was more to come. A lot more.

"The original arrest warrant was based on limited information and limited evidence; your addendum warrant is based also on that. The information we have now available is that the death of Seamus Carville was caused by industrial cleaning fluid and that is founded on expert testimony from not one but two specialist chemists. The original warrant on Seamus Carville's death outlined two possible causes of death; poison taken over a period that eventually caused heart failure and/or poison administered forcibly in a large dose during a single event. Neither theory now holds. I am satisfied that the premise of Seamus Carville by accident, consuming a substantive amount of cleaning detergent in a single event caused instant death is accurate or at the very least far more likely. Therefore, the continued detention of Michael McDonagh is no longer in the interests of justice."

"That is quite the speech, Mr. McDonald,' snarled Armstrong through teeth that would take a week to un-grit. He put his head close to the Magistrate and continued, he hoped to convey not just his anger and his contempt but also suggest the fire and brimstone he could unleash on these inconsequential people. "I am taking Michael McDonagh to Dublin, you can make your speech to the Chief Justice, he may listen to you. I will not." Armstrong turned to his men and shouted, "Is that car ready yet?"

O'Reilly who was still smarting from being implicitly called a culchie would now decide that this man from the north needed to be put in his place.

"Inspector Armstrong, when your car is ready, you may leave. But you will not be leaving with the prisoner. This is my police barracks, this is my town, this is my law. The defendant will return to the custody of Sergeant Nixon, for him to dispense the justice that his RM sees fit." He paused and with a half-smile looked at Special Branch leader.

"That is how it is going to work."

He paused again before adding with contempt dripping from every word.

"And no city boy arse is going to dictate to me what I do, and I don't care if he is from Dublin, or Belfast, or Timbuctoo."

"You know you will all be sacked for this," replied Armstrong trying to add a hint of dismissal to his voice.

"Will we? Well, let's see about that. Shall we?" O'Reilly was now enjoying the engagement. He signalled to his officer, "Have their car ready in ten minutes, they need to be on their way. Now gentlemen, whilst this resolves itself, may I suggest a cup of tea and a biscuit?" He looked at the new arrivals. "And as I believe we have visitors from America, you won't have had the opportunity to try our local soda farls. So much better than that of Ennis." He then turned to the Special Branch Inspector, "I am sure you will want to be on your way, it has been a traumatic twenty-four hours for you. Give my best regards to the Lord Chief Justice."

O'Reilly turned away and led what seemed like a small crowd to his office. It was not every day that he had another county Resident Magistrate, two visiting Americans, a professor, and of course, his brother-in-law to visit.

"Eric you are going to have to stay the night, Sadie will never forgive me if she knew you were here. You can phone Mavis and explain the situation, I'm sure a night without you will have her pining even more for your return."

Nixon raised his eyebrows, 'pining' would not be top of Mavis's list, he suspected.

All this took place under the volcanic eye of Inspector Armstrong. He would make sure this was not the last they heard of this, and he was now more suspicious that there was foul play with his tyres. How were these people on the same side as him? This would be the thought that he would smoulder on as they journeyed the remaining four hours back to Dublin.

27

That following evening there was an impromptu party at O'Herlihy's. The RM to the surprise of everyone made a brief appearance. He did not stay too long just in case a couple of the chaps who were on their drills decided to take a potshot at him, but he knew he was the hero of the hour. He had shown that British justice still mattered in the new Ireland.

And when you had the chance to be lauded as a hero, why would you not take it?

Michael had been thrown into the air by his fellow workers as they carried him down Main Street.

The full pub at 5 pm was so unusual that Jonjo decided to throw a 5% discount on all drinks. He was a generous man, a community man and this was his way of showing it. Mary nearly had a coronary herself, she laughed so loudly on hearing her Dad's sanctimonious announcement over the din.

Her only disappointment was Tim and Jack could stay only briefly for the celebration. Thomas Dillon had to be returned to Galway City. His job is done. Another blow of freedom for the soon-to-be Republic.

Tom was grinning ear-to-ear. Michael just looked relieved, both from no longer being under arrest, but also not being thrown into the air by his co-workers again. Even Maire stepped into the pub briefly but did not stay. She was looking for Eric Nixon to give him a big hug. But he would not be around until the weekend. It was likely he would have to refuse the hug anyway as it may upset Mavis's pining, should she ever find out.

Robert Kelly had decided to give the celebration a miss. His back was still painful and all he wanted was more painkillers and his bed. In hindsight, he decided, this was an adventure he could have happily missed. It had not helped his back.

However, there was a part of him that was secretly delighted. He had seen his son rise up. The torpor he had witnessed over the previous couple of years since he returned from the war had given way to thought and action. A man's life had been irrevocably changed because of his boy. This was what he knew Jack had done. His son was a natural leader who could rise above the directionless world that 1921 America had become. So as he lay in the bed looking up at the ceiling wishing for the tablets to start working their magic, he thought of his wife Anne. She would be looking down with pride on their boy, their son. And maybe she would be looking down with more than a hint of satisfaction for her husband. This adventure was a good move, it was helping them all recover from events that a sudden loss can bring.

He just wished the wife could have a word with St. Peter upstairs to help his back a bit.

The following morning saw an immediate return to routine, but things had changed. Sometimes events occur that nudge you in a direction, that deep down you knew you were heading towards.

For Tim Smith and Michael McDonagh, this was the case.

Michael had been profuse in his gratitude to the Kellys and the Smiths, but after breakfast, he asked to go for a walk with Jack. His restlessness was leading him to areas of which he had little understanding, least of all the consequences.

"Jack, when you are in a cell by yourself, thinking that only the worst can happen, you have these small gaps of sanity where hope appears, and you think about what you'll do when this is over. And that was all I could think about. So I'm gonna leave here."

"You're gonna' leave? To go where, to do what?" Jack queried.

"That's why we're having this walk, Jack," Michael smiled as he said it.

"I was thinking about England but having met you and your Da' I am now thinking further. America....or Australia, maybe even South Africa. But not here, I'll not amount to anything here. My energy will go into the wrong things."

"But what about your Mom, sorry I mean your Mammy?" Jack grinned as he said, "It will be difficult to leave her. And then there is Siobhán, she is sweet on you."

Michael nodded.

"I know that, and I have not talked to Tom yet on this, I'm hoping when I do, you could maybe help me a bit. And as far as Siobhán is concerned. I'm sweet on her, I will want her to go with me."

"This is big stuff, Michael. You deffo need to talk with Tom."

"Do you think America is big enough for me, Jack?"

Jack laughed loudly, "I'm not so sure there Michael, the way you took out those Doolin Hurley players, you'll frighten everybody." The laughter continued.

"Well, I'm strong, I can work. I'm not stupid, just a little naïve," Michael grimaced as he thought of the previous few days.

"Oh you'll be fine in America; you'll be fine anywhere. This is a small town, a small community. It must be difficult to welcome the world for a couple of weeks during the festival and then return to normal thereafter. I know, I couldn't live here."

"You better not say that to Mary," Michael turned the tables.

"Yeah, she's a great girl but I think Tim or your Tom are probably better for her in the long run."

"I'm not sure Tom thinks he's good enough." Michael sighed, before continuing, "Anyway this is about me, we can talk about you some other day. I'll have that chat with Tom but maybe have you nearby on that one. And then I'll go and speak with me Mammy," he looked earnestly at Jack and smiled, "And maybe I might need your Da's help with that one, as well."

"I'm going to London; I'm going to be a racer. I'll spend six months giving it a go at Brooklands near London and see if a team picks me up, if they do not I'll return here and take over the legal practice. I just cannot do it now Da' I need to do this first."

"So, do you have any idea how much this fantasy of yours will cost? Who do you think will be paying for this?" Paddy was very angry, this to him was another wild goose chase with no attainable objective. He could not understand why the boy could not settle down, marry Mary....even though Paddy was not too keen on the father, and enjoy a very comfortable life serving the needs of the people in County Clare.

"I need to do this, Da' nothing will have changed, if and when I return."

"A decent girl may have gone, son."

"How do you mean?"

"Mary will have gone, and you will be left with fine girls, but not princesses."

Tim nodded in agreement with his father, on this the old man was right. He needed to include Mary in his thoughts. He also needed a conversation with Jack.

As Robert woke from his slumber to discover his son's bed empty, he found himself thanking his wife in a manner he had not done for a while. His back felt so much better. She must have had a word with somebody.

They had been in Lisdoonvarna for a few weeks now as they were heading into October, it was time to go to other parts of the Island. First across to Wicklow & Wexford then up to Dublin before heading north to the Mountains of Mourne, before Belfast, thereafter, further north taking in the Giants Causeway and this strange thing he had been told about, called the Carrick-a-Reede bridge. He had been advised to buy insurance before walking across it.

Crokepatrick had been walked as had Benbulbin. Errigal could wait.

He believed he had witnessed his son leave the fecklessness that had been the hallmark of the previous years behind. The war, and the loss of his mother, he knew had an impact, but his generation 'just got on with things,' even when in truth he struggled.

But to see his son use his knowledge, lead from the front, as well as riding a *damn* horse. It was more than he could have hoped. They both had become closer, the humour between them which initially was stilted now ran seamlessly. It was supportive and cutting, condescending and fun in equal measure.

There had been a re-awakening in both men. Or at least Robert wanted to believe.

And then there was Mary.

If he could box her up and take her to Philadelphia, he would in a heartbeat. She was perfect for Jack. There was nothing for her in Lisdoonvarna, a girl like that should have more in her life than running the pub of that old sot of a father of hers. Although Robert did like Jonjo.

And then there was 'Oul Dympna....how would you explain her to the folks back home? What a character. Thinking about her he determined to walk up the hill and have another of the bizarre conversations, he knew she enjoyed some much. He laughed inwardly at the thought.

Yet there he was fifteen minutes later, leaving the house after ignoring the entreaties from Maire to have a 'wee cup of tea and a slice of soda bread,' he would return later for that, and indeed if Maire were to add a couple of eggs to the soda bread he would be her friend for life.

This. Thrilled. Maire.

Her heart missed a beat as he left with the promise of returning within the hour. The excitement of Michael's release, the knowledge that God did answer prayers or to be more precise, the Virgin Mary, our Lady of Fatima intercede on another woman's behalf for her son was more than manna from heaven.

God was indeed good and if he was now presenting her with a stylish fifty-something American man, then oh Lord, what would she be saying to Fergus in her prayers?

She would worry about that one later.

28

Robert Kelly waved at Siobhán as she stood at the door of her father's shop. Michael had promised to take her for a long unaccompanied walk at 1 pm and she was beside herself with excitement. Except, of course, there would be none of this 'unaccompanied' nonsense.

Willie O'Neil, the matchmaker, as part of the job specification, required appropriate chaperoning to ensure correct behaviour by the courting couples. He would be walking ten yards in front. This distance was deemed long enough to enable some privacy for the pair, but also close enough to pick up on any inappropriate discussion points. Willie's experience on these matters told him that you needed to keep a back-eye on the girls just as much as the boys when it came to these rituals.

For Siobhán, this was all moot. All she could think was would he propose or not....?

Either way, she would be rushing to see Mary afterwards to help with the interpretation of what he had said even if it was not a marriage proposal. No word, inflexion, or mannerism of

Michael would be left out when it came to relaying what he said. Such are the ways of youth.

Kelly made his way out of town and up to the twin wells, a certain bounce in his step. Life was good and to see 'Oul Dympna sat there with no customers made it even better. For him, at least.

"Dympna may I have a cup of your delicious life-preserving waters?"

She eyed him with suspicion.

"Are you taken with the drink?" She eyed him suspiciously, causing Kelly to smile, did she mean the water or alcohol? Was she being humourous?

At any rate, she was right, he needed to tone down his jolliness.

"It's been a great couple of days Dympna, I'm happy. I'm happy for the town, I'm happy for everybody. It's been a great finish to the festival."

"Aye, that it has."

Dympna reverted to form. Kelly just laughed.

"I would like to thank the spirits for helping."

"Wid' cha' now?"

"Aye, I would." Two could play the 'Aye' game thought Kelly, and he continued, "Well something was helping us with Michael. Surely?"

"Aye, you'd be right."

"Prayer, diligent work, and some good fortune would be things that come to mind."

"Wid' they now?"

"Well, yes the spirits could hardly have planned this."

"They did now."

"And how did they do that?"

'Oul Dympna shook her head and half smiled at Kelly. These people did not understand......how could they understand? How could they know that Maire's wish for her boys to find their places in life had encompassed more than prayer, how that sprig of heather when they together bathed in the stream at midnight calling out to Grainne, Queen of the Spirits to rid Michael of his demons. To find a proper role in life for Tom and then for Damian to come out of his shell. How could an American understand?

And she was right.

Robert Kelly decided the shake of the head was all the answer he was going to receive.

"I wish you well, Dympna, I wish you well." Smiling he waved as he walked away, it was time he headed to the pub. It must be near opening time.

Tim and Jack had walked up to the field with Tom early in the morning. He had agreed to let them do some back-breaking work. Both men, much to the surprise of Tom wanted the catharsis of manual labour before they embarked on the next phase of their lives.

Neither man had ever baled hay, so the first hour consisted of Tom showing them the correct procedure before allowing them to do it themselves. This caused much mirth amongst the other fieldhands. Tim Smith whilst a local had never sullied his hands at this type of work and Jack well.....he was the complete city boy and could rationalise in his mind how things worked on a farm but would have no clue in practice as to what it entailed. His dad, of course, would have had an opinion on that given where his father had learned the work ethic.

By the time they took a break at 11 am, the soft delicate hands of Jack and Tim were blistered, bleeding, and painful. And as for their backs..........

"I think Tom, we will call it a day at lunchtime, this is just too hard."

"Aw sure boys, you get used to it. We'll be harvesting shortly, now that really is hard work," McDonagh grinned at them both.

They both laughed.

Tom was in his element; this was his domain. Every field hand had a complete respect for him. They listened to him as he outlined the jobs for the day and were happy to accept any corrections he requested of them in their baling. He never shouted, he just simply led. For Tim and Jack, it was clear that he was wasted in this environment, yet he seemed relatively content. As he was so quiet by nature though, you could never be certain. When the three of them talked in the field, it was more Tom doing the talking. He outlined how the work was divided over the year, what it was really like when the weather was truly awful, and the satisfaction of a pint of stout at the end of the day. Albeit he did not really drink.

He took pride in what he did and those he worked with. Yes, it would be better if the land was owned by someone who lived in the area, but everybody was paid on time and there was always a Christmas bonus. Unbeknownst to his mother, he had put away enough money to buy his own cottage. There were worse ways to live, he had comfort, some wealth, and a community. He would not swap that for the bright lights of anywhere.

1 pm finally arrived for the non-country boys, who by that point thought they would be ruined for the rest of their lives as they looked at their hands. Never again. They would now head to the pub for the afternoon because by God they had earned it. At least in their minds. They bade farewell to their temporary colleagues knowing they would see them later in the same pub they were heading to now. So whilst the real men worked in the field, the unreal men would have two pints before heading home, having a wash and a nap in that order, and then returning to the pub for a post-work drink when the others had finished in the field.

The city slickers, breathed a sigh of relief as they trundled down the hill towards Lisdoonvarna.

"Nope, not for me. Once we've done the rest of Ireland, Fatima, and the Camino, I'll be happy to do anything that involves an office or a laboratory. Can you imagine how *awful*, Tom's version of *awful* must be? What must it be like in the winter?" Jack shook his head.

"Well, you should see our summers," Tim jocularly remarked to which they both laughed.

"Dad has agreed to fund me six months in London to try and make it as a racer," Tim announced to Jack. "And I think if I find a bit of work over there when I'm not racing, I can probably squeeze another six months out of it, So by this time next year I'll know if I am to be my Da' or a racer boy."

"I suspect you've tried your dad's patience somewhat."

"Well, *me mammy* is none too pleased either," he smiled.

"So what then of Mary? Is she in your thinking?" Jack cheekily inquired.

"Yeah, she is. But not at the forefront. I need to do this first." Before adding, "What would be the point in marrying her and having this eat away at me? And it would."

"Would you not be upset if someone came and swept her away from you? If Tom came in? Or dare I say a young good-looking war hero of an all-American boy. " They both began laughing at this.

"I guess, I would just have to go to *Amer-ree-kay* and shoot that *coun-ta-ree boy*," Tim responded in as bad an American accent as Jack's efforts on the Irish drawl.

"Thanks for marking my card on that one, Tim." Jack smiled.

They arrived at O'Herlihy's and were a little surprised to see Jonjo, Mary, and Robert huddled in the corner in deep conversation. They strode over to them but did note that whatever they were talking about, Mary seemed a little agitated, to say the least.

29

Robert had arrived at O'Herlihy's, and it was open for business. Several regulars were leaning against the bar, not talking to each other, more focused on their pint and their thoughts. What can they be thinking about? Or hoping? What plans could they be concocting? Robert wondered. He placed an order from Gerry for a Murphys, he found that to be more to his taste than the Guinness. Slightly less bitter. He noted Jonjo in the corner booth with Mary, their conversation seemed somewhat intense, so he thought it best to avoid eye contact.

Until Jonjo tapped him on the shoulder and queried whether he had a *'wee'* minute, there was something he wanted to discuss with him.' Robert was somewhat uncertain about what there was for discussion. Did he want a loan or something? At any rate, he picked up his pint and followed Jonjo over to where Mary was sitting.

"Sure, isn't Jack amazing," began Mary, "Without him, Lord knows what they would be doing with Michael now." The two men nodded in agreement, but Robert was not sure the intensity of the father and daughter discussion could be on 'what a great boy, Jack was.'

"Well, he did get a little help. Everybody played a role. The community played its role. Which is lovely, I'm not sure what would have happened in Philadelphia if there was a similar scenario."

"Why do you say that Robert?" Jonjo questioned, which slightly surprised Robert.

"Well, I guess....I'm not sure. Maybe we are a more money-motivated society....there was no money in the motivation here." He became slightly hesitant," I don't know....maybe I am wrong, maybe I am being a little unfair to my home city." Robert Kelly was now regretting his earlier answer, had he seriously just criticised Philadelphia and the city, he quite frankly loved? "I don't know what I am saying. At any rate, everybody deserves a pat on the back for this."

Jonjo and Mary smiled at the tongue-tied Robert.

"So why don't you stay here, if you like the community so much?" Jonjo gently teased. Robert found himself laughing.

"Yeah, I might just do that. Maybe set up a pub here, an American pub. With no liquor, that would work well." They all laughed out loud at the thought of a prohibition American pub in the West of Ireland.

"So anyways," Jonjo began, evidently happy to pluralise the 'anyway.' We were wondering what America would be like for a girl to travel to....or to be more precise, my beautiful, only, light of my life, the reason for my being....daughter?" He smiled broadly as Mary rolled her eyes in a manner to indicate this was one emotional guilt trip in public, too many.

"What Da' is saying, and saying badly is I want to have an adventure and I think I would like it to be in America. I'm promising him I will return and decide only after I return whether I want my life to be here....or," she paused, before looking at Jonjo, "....Or somewhere else."

Jack nodded in understanding, yet his mind was racing; was Mary asking him to push Jack towards her? Please, God, she was. Please, please God she was.

But she was not.

"The last few weeks," Mary began, "Have helped me see my future and if it is to be spent here in Lisdoonvarna, then I need to see something of the world first."

This was not quite what Robert was hoping.

"The thing is I could go to London, but I don't think that's far enough away from here. And Australia, well maybe that is just too far. I was thinking about America for maybe six months. So my question is do you think that's a good idea? And would I get in?"

"I would ensure you would get in." Robert smiled at Mary and then having seen Jonjo's glum expression decided that it would be useful to introduce a few caveats. "What I mean is, there are restrictions to entry now, but if you have a job to go to a sponsor then it is relatively straightforward. Particularly if that sponsor was a senior police officer in a major US city." Robert's modesty was underwhelming at this stage. Mary laughed, with even Jonjo managing a grimaced smile. He was about to lose his daughter for a period.

"Look, my brother runs a restaurant in New York, we can probably arrange for you to have a job there, this and a letter from me will probably be enough for the Consulate to give you a visa to go. There may be a few extra issues if you want to stay, but we can worry about that later."

"Well there you go, Da' that's the issue sorted."

"Is it now?" Jonjo was taking a different view.

"Yes, Da' it will only be for six months and then I will return here, I promise. But what I won't promise is what I will do after that." She looked at him hard, "It's what I'll be doing Da'." This girl was establishing a new law for Daddy to begin adjusting to, which unfortunately for Robert was not something he was picking up on.

"But you know Mary," he began with a concerned look that displayed no small degree of pomposity, "You are not getting any younger," and then added to his misread of the situation, "And you are such a very beautiful girl, you have a ready choice of suitors, do you have no wish to settle down?"

Mary reddened. It was something Jonjo had seen before and he was grateful that he was not about to be on the receiving end of the fusillade that was about to come Robert Kelly's direction, but fate took a hand and intervened.

Jack Kelly and Tim Smith walked into the pub and headed straight for their table.

30

"I hope we haven't interrupted anything," Jack breezily commented. The look on Mary's face indicated they had.

The look on his Dad's face suggested, some degree of gratitude as Robert had now worked out his '*compliment*' had fallen on stony ground.

"Oh nothing too much, your Da' is trying to get me married off, which makes a change from it being my Da' trying to get me married off........" She smiled, calming down as she did so.

"Well, he's been trying to marry me off for a while, so it's kind of an affliction he has. I want to invent a pill as I am certain he cannot be the only thoughtless 60-something-year-old father who has the same sickness. Maybe we could run some trials with him and Jonjo." They all laughed whilst Robert pretended to 'enjoy' a grimace.

"Look at our hands," Tim decided to move the conversation in his direction. "They were not made for field work."

"What were they made for then?" Mary laughed as she looked at him.

"Ah that would be tellin' now, wouldn't it?" Tim retorted before Jack brushed him aside in the hunt for a sympathy vote, which was not immediately presenting itself at the table,

"Well these hands were made for chemistry, but given their current state, it will be a few months before I can go near a test tube or Bunsen burner again."

"You poor, poor boys," Mary was struggling to dish out the desired sympathy.

"And let me guess you left Tom up there for the afternoon to just get on with it....He's the only man amongst ye," She smiled, but they could sense some mild seriousness and accuracy in her comment.

"Okayyyyyy, I think we should get ourselves a couple of pints and maybe return to the table in five minutes," Jack looked at Tim when he said this and raised his eyebrows at the same time.

"Boys, you're not going anywhere, I need your help." She signalled to Gerry, "Two pints for Jack and Tim," she paused and made the 'pour a pint' gesture to Gerry.

They were all working out what Jonjo had realised a while back; Mary actually ran the place.

"So I am thinking of going to America for a bit, what do you two think?" The boys looked at each other uncertain what to say, 'was she serious?'

"Oh, am I not allowed to have dreams? Am I allowed to think of things beyond being a lawyer's wife," she looked at Tim, "Or wait for the tall dark stranger to come in and steal me away?" The two younger men were now in the same position as the two older men. They were not sure where to look. She had said the 'what they were thinking part,' out loud. She then looked at both of them, well rather through them than at them. They fumbled for words before Jonjo rode to their rescue,

"I'm thinking Mary is not wanting a marriage proposal, she has a life to live," He sighed. "But you know something you're right. Go. Your Ma' will have wanted you to do it, your brothers would have wanted you to do it, and although I can barely believe I'm saying this.....I want you to do it." He paused before adding, "I might even join you." The half-smile that was breaking out on Mary's face then turned to a stern look at a father.

"Ah, that would be a 'no' then to that idea." The grins around the table told the other men, they could come up for conversational air.

"Mary, I think it's a great idea, and it's only for a short time as well, we will maybe be back in America before you return. You'll know what you'll want to do by then." Jack was putting down an early marriage marker while Tim, realising that he needed to put himself back *in the game,* thought it useful to update everybody on his plan for London and racing.

"So I'll either be a very rich racing driver or I'll be a lawyer here this time next year. I could then visit you all in America......." He hesitated, "And then of course I could take you back here to your Da,'" he was now doing the half-smile and looking at Jack as he said it. That was his marker put down.

Jonjo beamed. Robert bristled slightly; his son should not compete with what was the word that the police officer had used. 'Culchie.' Yes, that was the word and to Robert Kelly's mind, it was the appropriate word for this Irish boy racer.

"Good, well now that we've sorted all that out, we can focus on the finale night of the festival and see which of Willie O'Neil's hopefuls have been able to get across the line." She then pointed to the corner where the Matchmaker extraordinaire was huddled with the middle-aged English lady who had been at the McDonagh's hotel and Conor O'Shea, a farmer from near Doolin, who was never quite sure which town to support when it came to the Hurling. The look on

Willie's face and the closeness with which the couple were sitting indicated that his special skillset had once again worked its magic.

31

The concluding event of this year's festival was to be an open-air party down Main Street. It would start at 11 am and finish at 4 pm. This would enable travellers to depart in daylight hours with some chance of certainly arriving in Ennis for the late-night train to Dublin.

Various stalls had been set-up covering everything from sewing through to apple dunking. With the part closest to Jonjo's pub being where a band would play. Jonjo was nothing if not a master marketeer and in addition to the pub, two stalls had been set-up further down the street with Mary running one of them.

And after some mild bullying, Jack and Tim to the immense surprise of their fathers agreed to run the other one. Their boys had changed.

The band that had been selected was not designed to appeal to a younger age group. Too many bodhrán, fiddles, and flutes for the type of dancing that they would have wanted. This was just *too* family and whilst it enabled the Priest and the Nuns to have a jig themselves, the matchmaking target set would have to make do with drinking.

For Willie O'Neil, who had been pleased with his successes during the festival, this would be an opportunity to start preparation for next year. He would talk to the ones he felt were suitable matches for each other but yet had not been able to find the connection. He would try to understand why and note everything down, continuous learning was at the core of everything he did.

He was a believer.

He believed in love, in romance, in family. Whatever he could do to help others find the path, its path, he would do it in a heartbeat.

And who was to say that even in the last hours, the last minutes of the festival a union could not be found?

The dancing had seen all manner of shapes being cut, with Fr. Enda and Sister Joan seemingly enjoying a version of a 'Gay Gordon' that was somewhat different from that where it was invented across the Irish Sea. The Curates and Nuns looked on with both shock and disapproval. Was this appropriate? Were they not engaging in 'sins of the flesh?' Even if it was with the elderly and children? Fr. Joachim, the man who had delivered the sermon on the seven deadly sins was seen shaking his head, what was the world coming to?

Jonjo's bar was packed, and Mary's stall was packed, however, Tim and Jack were struggling. Initially, they attracted a big crowd. The locals wanted to hang out with the perceived wealthy boys, but their inability to serve the clientele quickly had now destroyed credibility to the extent that they were left shouting out to people as they passed by, whether they wanted a drink.

That is the thing about running a pub, even if it is only temporary, once your reputation has gone. It. Is. Gone.

As the day was drawing towards its end, the band began to play some of the more modern tunes, and this attracted the younger people back to them. All the songs they played were popular, just not to the standard of even Big P and his Baseliners. However, enough drink had been taken by the boys to make them more inclined to become involved. Or at least stand right on the edge of the sandy dancefloor and watch the girls dance.

Those who were now entwined in a courtship wanted the world to see how 'official' it all was, assuming that this gave them enhanced social standing.

A shriek went up from the middle of the ten couples dancing, which caused, the band to stop playing. Had someone hurt themselves?

It was Siobhán and she was crying. But crying with the biggest smile ever on her face. Michael had just asked her to marry him. This, despite having gone through a whole raft of possible answers with Mary only a few days before on what she would say if ever asked, she found them all dissolving into a simple 'yes.'

She then proceeded to leave the dance floor and pull the Dolan sisters to her to tell them the news. The band started up again, not entirely sure what the commotion had been, but the initial clearing in front was soon again filled with younger ones. Siobhán and the Dolans were busy rushing up to Mary to tell her the news. Then and only then would she look for her father.

This left Michael on his own, but his ear-to-ear grin said it all, he walked over to a smiling Tom who had prior knowledge of his intentions.

"So she said, 'yes' then?"

"Aye that she did, I was worrying a wee bit when she didn't say yes immediately, she started to cry so I thought I had said something wrong, but then she said yes, sure enough."

Well, Ma' is happy, she thinks you need to settle down, even if it's not here."

Michael nodded, they were joined by Siobhán's father, Rory who also had a smile on his face.

"I'm sure she'll get round to telling me sometime, but all the girls in the town have to be told first, apparently," he rolled his eyes. Daughters......

Tom had spent the afternoon moving amongst his fellow field hands and the three bars. He liked Tim and Jack but preferred the people he worked with. The comradery, the humour, and their way were what he was comfortable with. Racing cars, chemistry, and travel were not for him. He was happy for Michael and his mother who seemed beside herself with delight when her son had announced his intention.

They were joined by Robert Kelly who had spent the day being entertained by the middle-aged English lady, Conor O'Shea, and Maire in the pub. Lucinda had regaled them all with her visit to Fatima and how it had inspired her faith. So yes the Kelly's definitely would visit the Portuguese town to see the shrine and meet up with an old war friend of Jacks. They would hope there was enough English language spoken there to make it all workable.

As they talked, Siobhán returned with her cohort and threw her arms around her father,

"I'm so happy Da,' so happy." And then threw her arms around Michael, "I'm going to make you such a good wife." The two widowers looked at each other, could they ever find this level of happiness that seemed to come so naturally to the young, again? The question would remain unresolved in their minds but pondered upon.

The Dolans were keen to return to the dancing, but Deirdre hung back a little. She had brushed Tom's hand, but he had not reacted. She brushed it again, but still nothing. Her sisters grabbed a couple of Tom's friends and pulled them onto the floor, leaving Siobhán to manhandle Michael. Robert and Rory were engaged in deep conversation.

"You don't like the jigging around too much Tom, do ye'?" Deirdre laughingly suggested to Tom.

"Aye, I've two left feet, God didn't make me for it."

"Och, it's only a bit of movement." She held his forearm and looked into his eyes.

There had been a long conversation with Mary about Tom. Deirdre was shy and thought Mary had the choice with him and she could not compete with the beautiful Mary. Upon hearing of her plans to move away for six months, Deirdre felt this was an opening, yet somehow needed Mary's consent. It was as if she had some virtual control over the eligible men of a certain age in the town. Mary removed all those shibboleths; Tom was there for the taking if it was what Deirdre wanted.

Deirdre steeled herself, she put her hand on his other forearm. It was as though she was about to jump into the icy stream waters and let those spirits float over her body.

"Well look, Tom McDonagh, those two big left feet of yours are good enough for me.....and I'm in the mood for dancing."

A short distance away, a man was seen to be taking out his notebook.

The End

Research Notes

This is a work of fiction. However, it references real-life individuals. Gore Vidal, in his introduction to Lincoln, writes that placing history in fiction or fiction in history has been unfashionable since Tolstoy and that the result can be accused of being neither. He defends the practice, pointing out that writers from Aeschylus to Shakespeare to Tolstoy have done so with not inconsiderable success and merit.

I have mentioned several key real-life individuals and events in this novel. My intention, in the following section, is to explain a little more about their connection to this period and the story.

Throughout the book, I have used '*Fr*' to represent the Priest.

For consistency and respective on the differences between 'American-English' and 'English-English,' I have tried to ensure that English-English is used.

Having been steeped in this world for the first twenty years of my life, my memory proved stronger than expected. However, I enjoyed 'The Last Matchmaker' a book by Willie Daly, who is the matchmaker in Lisdoonvarna! I watched The Quiet Man again, not so sure it has aged that well, some scenes are frankly quite appalling. However, the timelessness of 'Going My Way' the 1944 Bing Crosby movie remains an inspiration when thinking about the charm religious side of things.

The second single biggest resource was Wikipedia, one of the greatest tools ever.

Irish Words/Myths Used

Aibell, Fairy Queen of Cailleach,
A guardian spirit who had a magical heart where it was said that once you heard it being played, you passed away. She was the daughter of Cailleach and following an altercation with her sister, Clodagh was turned into a white cat

Cailleach
This is a mythical land that could be in the West of Ireland or the West of Scotland depending upon which myths you choose to believe

Gráinne
Was the daughter of King Cormac and was part of a great love trilogy between Finn (King of the Fianna) and Diarmuid, her younger, truer love. The story is similar to Arther, Lancelot, and Guinevere.

Geis
This is an Irish curse, however, there are potential upsides to some of them, and they can be a gift, eventually. So not quite like the normal Witches curse.

Seachtair
Irish storyteller

Slainte (Pronounced Se-lon-cha)
Irish (Celtic) word when toasting a drink. Gaelic for 'Health.'

Irish Politics/Names Used

RIC
Royal Irish Constabulary, the national police force. Consisting of an equal number of Protestants and Catholics.

Black and Tans
Initially recruited into the RIC to bolster policing, their role became more paramilitary, and as many were unemployed, and ex-army from the war, they proved unsuited to the role. Hence atrocities were carried out, most notably in Balbriggan and Bloody Sunday. They were disbanded when a peace agreement was signed and were at that point disliked even by the regular police force.

John Redmond
He was the leader of the Nationalists in the House of Commons and had thought he had gained Irish independence following a deal with the Liberal Party in 1914. The war however delayed the law's implementation. So tactically, not wishing to be seen as anti-unionist, he requested Irishmen everywhere join the British Army 'for as far as the firing line extends.' In time he regretted it as it was becoming clear as the war approached its end that there would only be a very watered-down version of the original 1914 parliamentary bill.

The North-East part of the island would remain within Britain. He died in 1918 and his death led to Sinn Fein winning most of the Nationalist seats at the December 1918 election as his party began to fall apart.

IRB/IRA/Irish Volunteers

The Irish Republican Brotherhood had been in existence for fifty years and were as active in America raising money as they were in Ireland, 'training' men for an eventual war against British occupation. They were at the centre of the 1916 uprising with the Volunteers, but having initially failed to win support from the population, they were re-organised under the leadership of Michael Collins, effectively merging the Volunteers with the IRB for the War of Independence.

1916 Proclamation

This was a statement read out on the steps of the General Post Office in the centre of Dublin to the effect that the Irish people only could control the affairs of Ireland. Thereafter there was a bloody uprising which was put down by the British and saw the execution of the leaders.

Irish War of Independence

After the 1916 uprising, the political focus was on finding a settlement that could be agreed upon by all parties in Ireland; the Republicans, the Nationalists, the Catholic Church, the Unionists, the Protestant Churches, and finally the British. After much killing, a ceasefire was agreed upon in June 1921 with a peace accord signed in December of the same year. The fighting varied in intensity around the Island. County

Clare was relatively unscathed however, Tipperary and Cork were badly affected.

Croke Park Massacre/Bloody Sunday

Following an attack by Michael Collins that saw 14 members of British Intelligence killed in the morning, the Black and Tans were sent to Croke Park where a Gaelic football match was taking place to carry out a search and find operation. In the event, they opened fire, killing 14 people including one of the players, and wounding 60 others, including children. Support for the IRA increased sharply after the incident.

Derry/Londonderry

City in North West of the island which is referred to as Derry, if Nationalist (predominantly but not exclusively Catholic) of Londonderry, if Unionist (predominantly but not exclusively Protestant)

Miscellaneous

Culchie

The pejorative word applied to those who are more likely to live in the country, but has been used against those who are perceived to be of lower refinement.

Scallions

Irish descriptions for spring onions.

Soda Farl

Oatmeal cake made in a frying pan.

Bodhrán
Irish musical instrument resembling hand drum.

And Mentioned in the Story.........

John McCormack
A doctor based in the US established a link between smoking and lung cancer, before World War One.

Mary Harms, Robert Steel
Former diplomat for Great Britain, who uncovered widespread abuse of the indigenous people in Congo

Whiskey in the Jar, Brian Boru, Spiorad Cuchalain
The above was a popular folk song that received the 'punk' treatment by Phil Lynott's, Thin Lizzy in the 70s. Brian Boru was an Irish King who stopped the Vikings in the tenth century, and 'Spirit of Cuchalian' refers to a mythical Irish warrior hero.

Prologue to the 4th Secret of Fatima

March 6th 1922

It had turned midnight, the heavy cloud covering ensured no shadows would be seen. They crept up the hill at Cova da Iria, with the outline of the tiny Chapel, the Capelinha as it was called, being only vaguely visible, they needed to be quiet as several pilgrim tents had been pitched in the vicinity. The orders had been clear, avoid loss of life, so their reconnaissance over a previous couple of days had been to make certain everyone would see the outcome, but nobody would be injured.

In their minds and planning, the Republic needed to send out a message that all entities within Portugal were subservient to the state, and that included the Church regardless of what a few peasant children may have seen. It was important for the country to drag its peasantry into the twenty-first century and it was their duty as free-born Portuguese citizens to ensure that would happen.

The four men had travelled from their various destinations and had joined the pilgrims 'praying' at the newly built Chapel. Their intentions however were not to seek salvation, they were looking at the structure of the small Church and identifying which tree the Virgin Mary supposedly had appeared to a nine-year-old, an eight-year-old, and a six-year-old. What nonsense, but yet here they were because this nonsense had taken on a life of its own as witnessed by the many tents in the area set up by people who seemed unable to understand that it was for them to control their own lives, not some super unseen entity whose representatives on earth sought to usurp government power.

Paco, the leader – they only knew each other by first names, deemed it better that the group assembled, should not be overly familiar with each other.

They had spent an early part of the day applying oil to the hinges to stop the noise. One of the pilgrims, an older American man, thanked him for being so thoughtful. What a joke, how could one of the most powerful nations on earth produce people who believed these yarns? At any rate, he would enjoy the irony later, after he had shaved, and saw the artist's drawing in the press of a bearded man whom the police wanted to talk with, that would surely follow. Right now, the focus was on finding the previously identified clefts in the Church.

The four tightly packed parcels were placed carefully in the selected crevasses, one behind the twelfth station. Another irony. Paco signalled for the other two men to leave. The fourth man, Adao who was nearly local, placed a fifth device in the hole of the tree where an apparition was said to have taken place. He joined the three other men as they made their way to the waiting car, an Essex Touring mobile, which had been stolen a few days earlier. They would stand on the São Mamede hill, awaiting the fireworks. After that, they would head to Porto. Back to civilisation, boats headed to Rio de Janeiro and Belem in Brazil, and Angola, where they would stay for several months before returning to Portugal.

The pilgrims who were scattered around in the fields that surrounded the Chapel and those who had been able to pay the extra that would have been required to stay in the Pensions and Albergos that were springing up in Fatima may have had many expectations on what the following day would bring. However, they were snapped out of their dreams sharply as just after midnight the packages of the four men fulfilled their mission.

BOOM!

The night sky was lit up, and surrounding tents were shaken. In Fatima the few who had electricity found themselves stretching for the switches. People were awoken from their slumber. Was this an earthquake? Were they under attack? If so, by whom?

Windows were opened in the town, panicked shouting could be heard all around.

'It came from up the hill, I think. From the grotto. There is a fire burning, bring buckets, bring water.'

The pilgrims had already begun to deal with the fire, the open well was furiously having its bucket lowered and wound back up again. It was however next to useless, the fires that were burning at the Chapel would have to just burn themselves out. The efforts of the pilgrims and the villagers would make minimal impact. In their hearts they knew it, the pilgrims had not reached that point. Their attempts to put out the fires had become even more frantic.

By morning, it was clear that the Chapel had burned down. The entire village and the pilgrims were in shock. Fr. Ferreira inspected the smouldering carcass of the once religious shrine shaking his head, 'Why?' He kept murmuring to all and no one particular.

Jack and Robert Kelly looked on with the crowds in askance at what was before them, they both knew a man-made explosion when they heard one. This was not an accident.

"Why would anyone do such a thing?" Robert the father looked at his son in a state of mild shock.

"Who knows Dad, but you heard what Fr. Ferreira said and Paulo? They think it's the government or the Freemasons." Then Jack looked up to a small crowd forming near the tree where the apparitions had taken place.

"Let's see what is happening there," he motioned for his dad to follow him.

They walked further up the hill, where a few others had been having the same thought. Captain Paulo Coutinho once of the Portuguese Army was already examining the bark with the help of two younger men, who had levered him up to look inside a hole in the trunk.

"Yes, yes, there is something here. I can see a timer, but I can't hear anything. Everybody be quiet."

There was a kind of silence, but the noise from around the smouldering walls of the Chapel meant it was far from perfect.

"Ok, there's a bomb here as well, so let me get down, and let's put a cordon around the tree until somebody can look at this. His younger helpers quickly followed the instructions. What rope they had, they placed in the direction of the Church creating a twenty-metre gap.

"No one is to set foot past this point," the men posted themselves facing away from the tree and towards the Chapel where a few more people had begun walking toward the trunk.

Jack and Robert arrived and were reminded again that Captain Paulo Coutinho who had served his time in the trenches under British command during the war could speak

English as well as he did, something that was in thin supply within the region.

"There is a bomb in the tree," he sighed, "I don't suppose, you learned how to defuse these things where you were in France, Jack?" Coutinho hopefully smiled as he looked in the young American's direction.

"Well I did a bit, but that was a few years ago, and there was a war going on, don't you remember, Paulo?" He paused and half-smiled, not so sure given the events, a full smile was appropriate, "Did you see a fuse?"

"Yes."

"Well pull it out. It won't be going off if it has not gone off by now." Jack suggested matter-of-factly.

Coutinho looked at him with mild disbelief, his training in the army had been designed to avoid going near bombs.

"You do it, if you are so confident," Coutinho challenged Jack as if forgetting his request from a minute earlier.

Robert the father was somewhat concerned as with most parents his nearly thirty-year-old son, who had fought at the front in France, four years previously could not be expected to know such things and should therefore wait for the 'professionals.' This device however was miles away from any professional. The four National Guardsmen looked no older than children.

Jack clambered up the tree and dropped both his hands into the open piece of the bark where the bomb was located, he felt for the cord and gave it a strong tug. It came up, and with his left hand, he lifted it out of the hole and dropped it to the ground. Next, he put both his arms back into the bark and lifted the 'safe' bomb out. He smiled at the growing crowd.

"Tudo seguro agora." (All safe now).

This was greeted by a cheer and a slow handclap from the smiling Paulo.

Robert Kelly did neither, his heart had just undergone another special moment provided by his son.

"The police can hopefully use this and do some testing for things like fingerprints and likely suppliers," The father offered to Paulo, who was only half listening. Robert repeated his statement, as any former detective of the Philadelphian Police Department would when they wanted attention, now that his heart had moved down the scale to simply 'racing.'

Fr. Ferreira had joined the crowd and made himself the first to congratulate Jack.

"*é um milagre, é um milagre,*" he murmured into Jacks ear. Jack understood the word 'milagre' as 'miracle' so dispensed with translating the other words.

He smiled and looked across to Paulo and did a thumbs up.

The Priest repeated the action, before turning to Jack and in broken English and staring earnestly into his eyes spoke.

"This tree was not meant to exist and yet it still stands, if it is not a miracle, it is a mystery." He paused and looked at the three men, "Maybe, it is the fourth mystery of Fatima, and this is one we can see."

About the Author

Edward Murray lives with his family in the south of England. Although born in Ireland he has lived all over the world, from the USA to India (where he met and worked with Mother Teresa in Calcutta), and from Australia to Hong Kong. He attends Mass every week and regards himself more as a cultural Catholic rather anything else and is a big believer in a 45-minute Mass.........
His books try to convey humour with regards to 1920s Catholicism in what was the beginning of a sharp change to social mores after the war.

Acknowledgments

It is not possible to write a book on your own. There are contributions from so many people either directly or indirectly over the period. Listing them all would be an impossible task, but Barry Taylor, John Convery, and Ed Caddle require above and beyond appreciation. Thanks chaps.
Special mention also should be made to my long-suffering spouse and family who have been patient and put up with my occasional grumpiness when working on this project.

Printed in Great Britain
by Amazon